D0278193

THE FAMOUS FIVE DIARY

Here's your chance to plot the year ahead
with your favourite friends – the Famous
Five! In this unique diary, Anne, Dick,
George (Georgina), Julian and Timmy share
lots of their secrets and adventures with you.
There's even a recipe from Aunt Fanny and
a quiz from Uncle Quentin!

Make this year the best ever with
THE FAMOUS FIVE DIARY!

Enid Blyton, who died in 1968 at the age of 71 became, during her lifetime, Britain's best-loved and most popular author, and is still considered to have wielded a greater influence than any other author over children's writing in the post-war years. She loved young people, and wrote – 'for all children, any children, everywhere' – over 600 books, many songs, poems and plays.

Have the Most Adventurous Year Ever with

THE FAMOUS FIVE DIARY

Compiled by Mary Danby and based on the
characters created by Enid Blyton and
featured in all the FAMOUS FIVE
ADVENTURES

Illustrated by Kate Rogers

KNIGHT BOOKS
Hodder and Stoughton

Photoset by Rowland Phototypesetting Limited, Bury St Edmunds, Suffolk. Printed and bound in Great Britain for Hodder and Stoughton Paperbacks, a division of Hodder and Stoughton Limited, Mill Road, Dunton Green, Sevenoaks, Kent TN13 2YA (Editorial Office: 47 Bedford Square, London WC1B 3DP) by Cox and Wyman Limited, Reading, Berks.

ISBN 0-340-42834-1

JANUARY

Jan 1

The first month of the year is named after the Roman god Janus, who was the god of 'doors and beginnings'.

Many people celebrate this fresh start by making New Year Resolutions. If the Famous Five were to write down their resolutions, what do you think they might put?

Jan 2

I resolve to control my quick temper and be quiet when my father is working.

I resolve to solve all the mysteries I can.

I resolve to try not to be hungry *all* the time.

I resolve to be extremely brave.

Woof woof! (Which probably means, 'I resolve to find the bone I buried last week.')

5

Jan 3

Why not list your own resolutions here, then you can check throughout the year to see how many of them you've kept!

I resolve ....

....

....

Jan 4

....

There was a young lady from Diss,
Who thought skating was absolute bliss;
Till love turned to hate,
When she slipped on a skate
And finished up something like this!

Jan 5	Jan 6

January 6th is the *Feast of the Epiphany* – the celebration of the visit of the Three Wise Men to the baby Jesus at Bethlehem. It's also known as Twelfth Night, which is the traditional time for taking down Christmas decorations. In some countries gifts are exchanged on this day rather than at Christmas.

Would you like to know how to grow your own mistletoe?

 Yes, I would.

Jan 7

Take down your sprig of mistletoe and hang it carefully somewhere cool to ripen the berries. At the beginning of April I'll tell you what you have to do next.

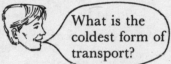 What is the coldest form of transport?

 A b-b-b-icicle!

Jan 8

January 8th: Two famous pop singers share this birthday – Elvis Presley and David Bowie.

It can be very cold in January, with the ground frozen for days on end. Wild birds have difficulty in finding enough food, so try Anne's recipe for **Bird Cake**. Cut off a piece each day and put it out for the birds. They'll love it!

1. Melt a large lump of lard in a saucepan. (*Don't get it too hot*, or it will spit – it just needs to be warm enough to become liquid.)

2. Now stir in any of these:
   Left-over breadcrumbs or cake crumbs
   Stale bread (cut into small pieces)
   Nuts of any kind (*except salted ones*)
   Dried fruit
   Porridge oats
   Left-over cereal
   Rosehips
   Rowan berries.

3. Stir the mixture well, then spoon it out of the saucepan into a cake tin. Press it down firmly and leave it in a cold place to set before turning it out on to an old plate.

Jan 9

Dads Birthday

Jan 10

Jan 11

Brighten up the dark winter days by painting your wellies. Use acrylic paint (which you can buy from hardware and hobby shops), but *be extremely careful with it* – once on, it's hard to get off. You'll need white spirit for cleaning your brush.

Here are some ideas you might like to copy:

Jan 12

Jan 13

Who or what might have made these strange marks in the snow?

Keepers is a game you can play while sitting round the fire. Julian might begin by saying, for instance, 'Who keeps cats?', and Dick might answer 'Fred'. Then Dick asks, 'Who keeps bees?' and George replies, 'Leslie'.

What are they doing? Well, a cat has four legs, so Dick has

Jan 14

to say a name beginning with F. For a bird (two legs), the name must begin with T, for an insect (lots of legs), it must start with L, and for a fish (no legs), with an N. The first person to say a suitable name scores a point and asks the next question. You may not use a name more than once. Keep score with a pile of buttons or matchsticks, and pick one up every time you gain a point.

Jan 15

Be safe on the roads.
Remember:
1. Wear something light at night.
2. If there's no pavement, always walk facing oncoming traffic.
3. Learn the Green Cross Code.

Last winter during the dark evenings I dressed all in white so that the traffic would see me.

Did that keep you safe?

No – I was nearly knocked down by a snow plough!

Jan 16

GOT NO BAG

Rearrange these letters to form the name of something that can carry you from top to bottom!

10

If you're lucky, you might see a snow bunting. They come from the Arctic to visit Britain during the winter. A snow bunting is about 16 cms long and has brownish plumage, with white underparts and black wing tips.

Jan 17

Jan 18

Jan 19

Knock knock

Who's there?

Jan

Jan who?

Janoo-ary the nineteenth

Did you know that in the Jewish religion, the New Year begins in the autumn?

11

Which lead leads to Timmy?

Jan 20

Jan 21

Do you believe in astrology? Some people say that your personality is governed by the date of your birth, and that people born under a certain sign of the zodiac will show the same characteristics. For instance, those born under the sign of Aquarius (January 21st to February 18th) are supposed to be sensitive, shy types, easily hurt. (Like Marybelle Le Noir, in *Five Go to Smuggler's Top*.)

Jan 22

Mrs Sanders lives at Kirrin Farmhouse. The Famous Five love to visit her – *and* there's always something tasty on the stove. Here's her recipe for **Farmhouse Soup**:

You will need:
450g potatoes
25g butter
1 medium-sized onion
1 pint water
1 beef stock cube

1. Peel and thinly slice the potatoes and onion.
2. Melt the butter in a saucepan and then add the potatoes and onions. Cook them on a low heat, with the lid on the pan, for 10 minutes. The potatoes should then be soft.
3. Add the water and the stock cube crumbled.
4. Bring to the boil and simmer gently for about 20 minutes.
5. Push the soup through a sieve, or chop it finely in a blender or food processor.
6. Serve hot, with lots of crusty bread!

Jan 23

Jan 24

Write down the first names of these famous people. The first letters of each name spell the name of a food which, cooked and chopped up, can be sprinkled on the soup.

____ Reynolds

_____ Christie

_____ Chaplin

_____ Cromwell

____ Edmonds

The end of January sees the beginning of the *Five Nations Rugby Championship.* The countries involved are England, Scotland, Wales, Ireland and France.

The game of rugby football was invented almost by accident in 1823, when William Webb Ellis, a football-playing pupil at Rugby School, in Warwickshire, picked up the ball and ran with it!

Jan 25

Jan 26

Jan 27

Book Quiz

1. Which famous public school was the setting for *Tom Brown's Schooldays?*
2. What did Willie Wonka make in his factory?
3. How many dalmatians did Dodie Smith write about?
4. In *The Jungle Book,* what is Kaa?
5. Whose books feature Hal and Roger and their search for wild animals?
6. Which girl detective is a friend of the Hardy Boys?

Jan 28

If you lost Timmy, would you put an advertisement in the paper?

Jan 29

Don't be silly! Timmy can't read.

Try this tongue twister:
Julian and George share jokes in January!

Make a Year Book

Collect newspaper articles, pictures etc. of important occasions and people in the news. These could include sporting events, royal weddings, news about the area where you live, items on pop stars, TV programmes, and so on.

Amongst all this, make a note of happenings in your own family, like births, deaths and marriages, holidays, prizes won, exciting news. Stick all this in an album, along with photographs, theatre programmes, bits of confetti – any kind of souvenir you can think of.

When you look back at your finished scrap book you'll be amazed at what an interesting year it's been!

Jan 30	Jan 31
	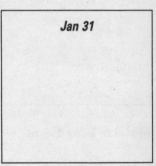

Answers to January puzzles:
Page 9: A man with a wooden leg pushing a wheelbarrow. Page 10: TOBOGGAN. Page 13: BACON (Burt, Agatha, Charlie, Oliver, Noel). Page 14: 1. Rugby School. 2. Chocolate. 3. A hundred and one. 4. A snake (a rock python). 5. Willard Price. 6. Nancy Drew.

FEBRUARY

February is the shortest month of the year, with just 28 days – or is it 29? Do you know the old rhyme?

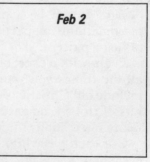

Thirty days hath
 September,
April, June and November;
All the rest have thirty-
 one,
Excepting February alone,
And that has twenty-eight days clear
And twenty-nine in each leap year.

The reason for this odd arrangement is that the earth goes once around the sun every 365.25 days. This is called a solar year. A calendar year is normally 365 days, but every fourth (or 'leap') year we have to slow down by adding one extra day, in order to keep pace with the solar year.

To find out if this year is a leap year, simply divide the year by 4. If it can be divided evenly, it's a leap year. (If the year ends in 00, however, you must divide by 400.)

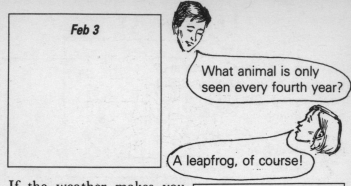

Feb 3

What animal is only seen every fourth year?

A leapfrog, of course!

Feb 4

If the weather makes you want to stay indoors, you might like to try making a collage. A collage is a collection of all sorts of bits and pieces, stuck on to a background to make a kind of design. It can be a picture of something in particular, or just a pattern.

Begin with a sheet of stiff card or paper. Now collect all the things you want to stick on to it. These could include old Christmas cards, sweet papers, bus tickets, bits of ribbon, magazine pictures, and so on. See how many interesting or unusual things you can find.

Feb 5

Cut each piece into whatever shape you want, then arrange all these on the paper, overlapping the pieces.

Now stick them down one by one, using a glue stick.

You can frame your picture by mounting it on a larger sheet of card in another colour, and hang it by taping a length of string firmly to the back.

Feb 6

February 6th is the anniversary of the day Queen Elizabeth II became queen. In 1952, news of the death of her father, King George VI, was brought to her while she was on holiday in Kenya, watching the wild animals at a place called Tree Tops. She was crowned sixteen months later.

Cruft's Dog Show is held on the second weekend in February. It was started in 1886 by Charles Cruft, a London dog breeder, and is now held every year at Earls Court.

The Supreme Champion at Crufts is always a very well-bred dog, but

Feb 7

whatever kind of dog you have, it should be properly looked after.

A dog needs his own bed, and shouldn't really be allowed to sleep on a human's bed (even though Timmy sometimes sleeps on George's bed). He should have his own basket or bed in a warm place, away from draughts.

Adult dogs need only one meal a day, and the amount of food you give them should depend on their size. Obviously, a big dog like Timmy would need more food than a Pekinese, for example. A balanced meal would contain meat or fish mixed with dog biscuits or cereal and perhaps some added vitamins. Make sure that a bowl of fresh water is available all the time.

A healthy dog is full of energy, and has bright eyes and a cold, wet nose. If he seems unwell, you must take him to see the vet. He should in any case visit the vet as a puppy, to be inoculated against serious diseases, then every year for booster injections.

Your dog must have regular exercise, no matter what the weather is like, otherwise he will become bored and

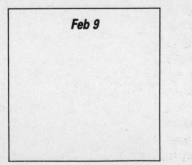

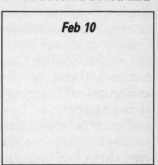

destructive. Lucky Timmy gets plenty of exercise when he joins George and her cousins on their adventures.

A happy dog is well-trained, and the most important part of the training is always to mean what you say! Don't tell your dog to sit and then give up when he won't obey you. Next time it'll be even harder. Dogs can easily understand a few basic words of command and will enjoy showing you how obedient they can be. If your dog disobeys you, don't hit him. Say 'No!' very firmly, then reward and encourage him when he gets it right.

Pancake Day (Shrove Tuesday)

Shrove Tuesday falls on a different date each year, because it is always forty days before Easter, but it usually comes in February. The following day, Ash Wednesday, is the beginning of Lent – a traditional period of fasting. In medieval times, no meat was eaten from Ash Wednesday to

Feb 11

to Easter Sunday, and on Shrove Tuesday people made pancakes which they filled with all the left-over meat in the house.

Nowadays, of course, we make Shrove Tuesday pancakes just for fun. Here's **Aunt Fanny's Pancake Recipe**:

You will need:
4 heaped tablespoons flour
1 egg
284 ml milk
Oil or lard for frying

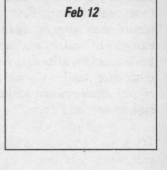

Feb 12

1. Mix the flour, egg and milk to a smooth batter – no lumps! (Use a large bowl and wooden spoon, or a food mixer.)

Feb 13

2. Heat a very small amount of lard or oil in a heavy frying pan.
3. Pour a tablespoon of batter into the pan and swirl it around.
4. Half way through cooking, when the underside is golden brown, turn the pancake over – toss it if you're feeling brave!
5. Serve it with lemon juice and sugar, jam, or ice-cream.

February 14th is *St Valentine's Day*.

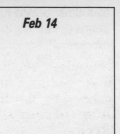

Feb 14

St Valentine was an Italian bishop who lived nearly two thousand years ago. Why he is regarded as the patron saint of lovers isn't clear, but in the 16th century it became the custom to send cards and presents anonymously to one's sweetheart on this day.

If you want to make a Valentine card, you might like to cut it out in the shape of a heart. Here's an easy way.

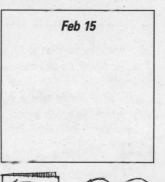

Feb 15

Fold your card or paper in two, then draw on it a shape like a cup handle. Keeping the card folded, cut out the shape. When you open the paper you'll have a perfect heart!

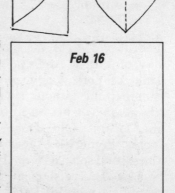

Someone who didn't receive any Valentine cards was Helen Morrison, who lived in Manchester in 1727. She placed the first ever 'lonely hearts' advertisement in a newspaper – the *Manchester Weekly Journal* – in the hope of finding a man friend. Sad to say, the Mayor of Manchester

Feb 16

was so shocked he had her placed in a lunatic asylum for four weeks!

Feb 17

Name the Sender

Which one of the Famous Five has sent this card?

This VALENTINE is sent from me. I'm hidden in it – can you see?

In February, when it snows,
I wear thick socks inside my
toes;
Glow and tingle like a bird,
My scarf flies out upon my
word.

Can you make sense of my nonsense rhyme?

Feb 18

February 19th is the birthday of Prince Andrew, the Duke of York. You may remember the famous rhyme about one of his ancestors, the Grand Old Duke of York. Frederick Augustus, the second son of George III, was made a bishop at the age of six months! Later, as

Feb 19

Duke of York, he became Commander-in-Chief of the British armed forces, but met with little success in his campaigns. Perhaps that's why the rhyme presents him as a rather silly fellow, always marching his men up and down hills!

Feb 20

The grand old Duke of York,

He had ten thousand men,

He marched them up to the top of the hill

And he marched them down again.

If you were born between February 19th and March 20th, you come under the star sign PISCES, which is the Latin for fish. Pisces people are supposed to be dreamers, forever wanting what they can't have! They are also romantic and imaginative. Famous Pisceans include Elizabeth Taylor and George Harrison.

Another type of fish altogether is the piranha. It's a small, freshwater fish from South America, and its name means 'fish with teeth'. They are great munchers, and a group of them is said once to have eaten a complete horse – and its saddle – in five minutes!

Feb 21

25

If you go walking or climbing in this cold, wet month, *you should be well prepared*. The weather can change for the worse surprisingly quickly! Try **Julian's Expedition Quiz** for February:

1. Is it better to wear one really good thick sweater or several thin ones?
2. What is a cagoule? rain coat
3. If you are climbing in the rain, should you wear rubber boots or leather ones? rubber
4. Should a rucksack be carried high on your back, or resting on your hips.
5. Why are chocolate, nuts and raisins good to take on a journey?
6. Why is it important to wear a hat on a cold day?
7. How can snow keep you warm in an emergency?
8. If you heard a whistle blown six times in one minute, followed by one minute's silence, then six again, and so on, what would this mean?
9. What colour flag is a recognised signal for help?
10. If you had to leave an injured friend while you went for help, what's the most important thing you could do for them?
11. You are lost and have no compass. What everyday object can help you find your way?
12. Which does your body need most – food or water?

Feb 22	*Feb 23*

Remember, before setting out on an expedition, always tell a grown-up exactly where you plan to go.

Feb 24

Feb 25

Why is February the shortest month?

Because all the others are longer!

Why did the snowman shed a tear?

Because he felt a little thaw.

Timmy, what is the opposite of smooth?

Er – ruff!

Feb 26

Feb 27

Feb 28

Feb 29

Answers to February puzzles:
Page 24: Anne (V**A**L**E**N-
T**I**N**E**).
Page 24:
In February, when it snows,
I wear thick socks. Inside,
  my toes
Glow and tingle. Like a bird
My scarf flies out. Upon
  my word!
Page 26: 1. Several thin ones,
as warm air will be trapped
between them. 2. A long,
lightweight type of anorak. 3.
Leather ones. Rubber soles
might make you slip. 4. High
on your back. 5. Because they
are easy to carry and will give
you energy quickly. 6. Because body heat rises and is
easily lost if your head is not
covered. 7. You can build a
shelter out of it. 8. Someone
needs help. 9. White. 10. Try
to keep them as warm and
sheltered as possible. 11.
Your watch. Point the hour
hand to the sun. Mid-way between the hour hand and 12
o'clock is North. 12. Water.

MARCH

Until 1752, March was considered to be the first month of the year. In Anglo-Saxon times it was known as *Hlyd monath* – the stormy month.

March 1st is *St David's Day*. Born in the 6th century AD, the patron saint of Wales was the son of a prince. He became the first abbot of Menevia (now St David's, in Dyfed), and his emblem was a dove.

Did you know that the border areas between England and Wales are called the Marches? (It's not because they're marshy, but because they mark the boundary.)

Mar 1

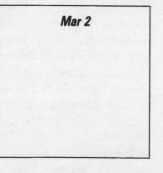

Mar 2

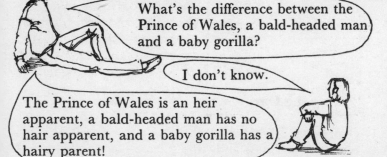

What's the difference between the Prince of Wales, a bald-headed man and a baby gorilla?

I don't know.

The Prince of Wales is an heir apparent, a bald-headed man has no hair apparent, and a baby gorilla has a hairy parent!

29

March is a music month, with birthdays for Shakin' Stevens (4th), Elaine Page (5th), Liza Minnelli (12th), Andrew Lloyd-Webber (22nd) and Elton John (25th).

Each spring, the Boat Race takes place on the River Thames. Rowing crews from Oxford and Cambridge universities compete over a course of nearly 7km between Putney and Mortlake.

The crews are called 'eights' and consist of eight oarsmen and a cox. The boat, which is very light and narrow, is known as a 'shell'. The oarsman at the front of the boat is called the 'bow', and the one nearest the stern and facing the cox is called the 'stroke'. He sets the rate of striking for the rest of the crew. The cox, of course, is the only one who can see where they're all going, so he operates the rudder.

Taking the Oars

George has a boat which she rows to Kirrin Island. She knows a lot about rowing.

Mar 3

Mar 4

Mar 5

Mar 6	
Mar 7	

Do you? Which of these statements are true, and which are false?

1. The left side of a boat is called the starboard side.
2. Oars are held in place by rowlocks.
3. The top edges of a boat are the gunwhales.
4. A rope attached to the bow of a boat is called a pointer.
5. A keel helps to keep a boat stable in the water.
6. To 'ship' the oars is to lose them overboard.
7. You should keep to the left of a green marker in the water.
8. A baler is used for tying up a boat.

On Kirrin Island sits the ruin of Kirrin Castle, where the Famous Five often have adventures. What do you think it looked like before it fell into disrepair? Here's all that's left of it – why not draw the rest in as you think it might once have been.

There are many castles still standing. Perhaps you've visited some. Have you spotted any of these features?

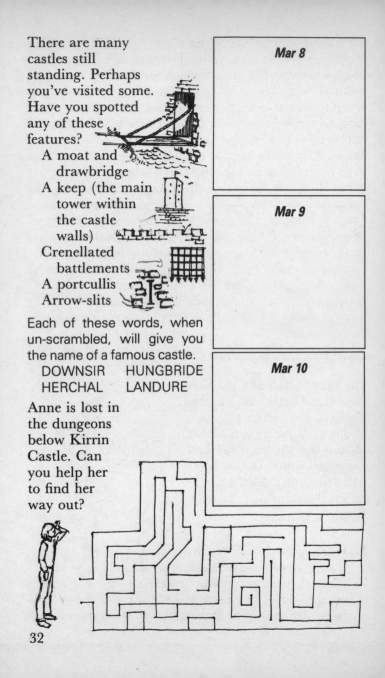

- A moat and drawbridge
- A keep (the main tower within the castle walls)
- Crenellated battlements
- A portcullis
- Arrow-slits

Each of these words, when un-scrambled, will give you the name of a famous castle.

DOWNSIR HUNGBRIDE
HERCHAL LANDURE

Anne is lost in the dungeons below Kirrin Castle. Can you help her to find her way out?

Mar 8

Mar 9

Mar 10

32

Mothering Sunday falls on the fourth Sunday in Lent. Many years ago it was the day when children who had left home to work as servants or farm labourers were allowed to go home to visit their mothers. The custom now is for children to give their mothers presents or cards on this day. It's often called Mother's Day.

Mar 11

Most mothers love to receive home-made presents. George knows that Aunt Fanny loves chocolate truffles, so she sometimes makes them for her as a surprise. Here's her recipe:

Mar 12

Chuffles *(by George)*

You will need:
125g sweet biscuits (such as digestives)
1 tablespoon golden syrup
1 tablespoon hot water
25g margarine
50g chocolate
1 teaspoon almond essence
Chocolate 'hundreds and thousands'
Paper sweet cases

1. Use a rolling pin to crush the biscuits. Place these in a large bowl with the golden syrup and hot water.
2. Melt the margarine and chocolate in a saucepan over a *gentle* heat, then add them to the bowl and beat the mixture thoroughly ('Until your arm

33

'aches,' says George). Stir in the almond essence.

3. Wait about 40 minutes until the mixture is cool, then shape it into small balls and roll them in the hundreds and thousands.

4. Place each chuffle in a paper case and arrange them in a box or basket.

Uncle Quentin's March Quiz

1. Which animal is said to be 'mad' in March?
2. In which book did the four March sisters first appear?
3. What does 'M.Arch.' after someone's name mean?
4. An army is said to march on its . . . what?
5. What is the husband of a marchioness called?
6. What sweet substance used to be called march-pane?
7. Edward Elgar, John Philip Sousa, Frederick Delius, Eric Coates – which one of these was not famous as a composer of marches?
8. In Shakespeare's play, who was told to 'beware the Ides (15th day) of March'?

Mar 13

Mar 14

Mar 15

Mar 16

Mar 17

March 17th is *St Patrick's Day*. The patron saint of Ireland lived over 1500 years ago and brought Christianity to that island. His emblem is the shamrock, which is worn by Irish people all over the world on St Patrick's Day.

The shamrock, which gets its name from the Gaelic word for clover, is a three-leaved plant. Can you find a four-leaved clover among the shamrock?

March 18th is the birthday of snooker player Alex 'Hurricane' Higgins.

Snooker is a game derived from billiards – a very popular pastime among British officers in India over a hundred years ago.

Each ball colour has a different value. Pocketing a red ball

Mar 18

scores just 1 point. Can you put the others in the right order of value, from 2 points to 7?

35

Mar 19

One of the greatest billiards and snooker players of all times was Joe Davis, who was world champion from 1927–1946. More recently, Steve Davis (no relation) has frequently won the snooker crown.

Why was the snooker player accused of theft?

Mar 20

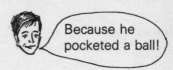

Because he pocketed a ball!

Here's another kind of ball game, which you can play with marbles on a hard floor or playground.

Use chalk to mark out an area about 1.5 metres wide. Each player must have his own section of the boundary.

In the centre, place a small heavy object, like a stone. Divide the marbles evenly between the players.

Players now take turns to roll a marble at the stone, keeping their hands outside the boundary. If a player succeeds in hitting the stone, he may then take back his own marble, plus any others left inside the boundary. A player may keep any marble that crosses his own part of the boundary. The winner is the player who ends up with all the marbles.

March 21st is the *First Day of Spring*. It's the time of the spring equinox, when the centre of the sun is above the horizon for the same length of time that it's below it, making night and day of equal length.

> **Mar 21**

The new star sign is ARIES – the ram. People born between March 21st and April 20th are said to be go-getters. They're strong and sometimes pushy, but a bit disorganised. Famous people born under this sign include Hans Christian Andersen, Marlon Brando, Penelope Keith and Neil Kinnock.

Linkword
What word can be joined either to the beginning or end of each of these words?
WATCH ONION BOARD
OFF FEVER

> **Mar 22**

At this time of year, hares can often be seen running wildly around the fields and 'boxing' with each other. It's their breeding season, and their excitable behaviour is the origin of the expression 'mad as a March hare'. (Timmy sometimes chases hares, but he has yet to catch one!)

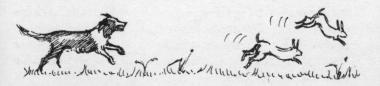

Lewis Carroll wrote about a mad March Hare in *Alice's Adventures in Wonderland*:

Mar 23

'Alice sat down in a large arm-chair at one end of the table.

'"Have some wine," the March Hare said in an encouraging tone.

'Alice looked all around the table, but there was nothing on it but tea. "I don't see any wine," she remarked.

'"There isn't any," said the March Hare.

'"Then it wasn't very civil of you to offer it," said Alice angrily.'

Mar 24

The planet Mars is the fourth planet from the sun. Like March, it is named after the Roman god of war – apparently because of its red colour. Sometimes it comes as near as 34 million miles (or 55 million kilometres) to the earth!

Mars has two very small satellites called Phobos, meaning fear, and Decimos, meaning panic.

It's cold on Mars, just −5°C, and the atmosphere is hazy. In 1965, when the American 'Mariner 4' spacecraft sent back close-up pictures of Mars, craters could be seen, just like those on the moon.

Mar 25

Planet Puzzle

Can you name the planets as they spread outwards from the sun? Here are some clues to help you:

The Sun

M e s c r e y (a liquid metal)

V e v n s (goddess of beauty)

E a r t h (you're on it)

M a r s (chocolate bar)

J u p i t e (ruler of the gods)

S a t u r n (ringed planet)

U r a n s (uranium was named after it)

N e p t u r e (sea-god with trident)

P l u t o (Disney dog)

Mar 26

Mar 27

Why is an astronomer like a boy who keeps bumping his head?

Because he's always seeing stars!

39

At this time of year, the Grand National is run at Aintree, near Liverpool. It's the world's most famous horse race over jumps, with thirty fences, including Becher's Brook, Valentine's, Canal Turn and the water jump, which is nearly 5 metres across. The best-known National winner is Red Rum, who won the race three times.

Mar 28

According to Scottish legend, the last three days of March are supposed to have been borrowed from April, and are therefore called the Borrowing Days. There's a rhyme about it:

March borrowed from Averil
Three days, and they were
*   ill.*

The one was sleet and the other was snow,
And the third was the worst that e'er did blow.

Mar 29

Mar 30

Mar 31

Answers to March puzzles:

Page 31: 1. False – it's the port side. 2. True. 3. True. 4. False – it's a painter. 5. True. 6. False – it's to bring them into the boat. 7. True. 8. False – it's for removing water from the bottom of the boat. Page 32: Windsor, Edinburgh, Harlech, Arundel. Page 34: 1. The hare. 2. 'Little Women'. 3. Master of Architecture. 4. Stomach. 5. A marquess. 6. Marzipan. 7. Frederick Delius. 8. Julius Caesar. Page 35: Yellow (2), green (3), brown (4), blue (5), pink (6), black (7). Page 37: Spring. Page 39: Mercury, Venus, Earth, Mars, Jupiter, Saturn, Uranus, Neptune, Pluto.

APRIL

Everyone knows that April 1st is *April Fool's Day*, but did you know that in France an April Fool is called a *Poisson d'Avril* – an April Fish!

Have fun playing tricks on everyone today, but don't forget that if you play a trick after 12 noon, the joke's on you, and you're the April Fool!

Apr 1

Apr 2

Apr 3

Over a hundred years ago, the poet Robert Browning, who was living in Italy at the time, wrote longingly about April in his poem 'Home-thoughts from Abroad':

Oh, to be in England
Now that April's there,
And whoever wakes in
England
Sees, some morning unaware,
That the lowest boughs and
the brushwood sheaf
Round the elm-tree bole are
in tiny leaf,
While the chaffinch sings on
the orchard bough
In England – now!

Remember I told you in January about growing your own mistletoe?

Yes – here are the ripened berries. They're quite dry and shrivelled. What do I do next?

Slit the bark on the underside of an apple, hawthorn or pear tree branch. Push two berries in, and cover them with clay or plasticine. Mistletoe produces berries only on female plants, so it's best to try growing several plants, to increase your chances of success.
Let's come back in September and see if we've been lucky.

43

Easter, which commemorates the Resurrection of Christ, is the greatest of all Christian festivals. It's a movable feast, which means it isn't celebrated on the same day each year. It always falls on the Sunday following the first full moon after the vernal equinox (March 21st).

> **Apr 4**

The name Easter is said to come from 'Ostera' – a goddess whose feast was celebrated by the Saxons in the spring.

The custom of giving each other Easter eggs, as symbols of rebirth, life and fruitfulness, is very ancient and widespread, especially in Europe.

The biggest-ever chocolate Easter egg was three metres high and contained nearly half a tonne of sweets and chocolate!

> **Apr 5**

> **Apr 6**
> mums birthday

Where did you get that nice Easter tie?

What makes you think it's an Easter tie?

It's got egg on it!

44

Apr 7

The most precious Easter eggs in the world were made by Carl Fabergé, goldsmith to the Russian royal family at the turn of the century. His Easter eggs were ornate and fanciful, decorated with jewels and full of intricate surprises.

Apr 8

You can decorate your own boiled eggs for breakfast on Easter Sunday. Draw faces on them, using waterproof ink before boiling, or any felt pens if the eggs are dry.

Apr 9

A fascinating fact: Every circus clown has his own special face design, which no other clown may copy. To register his clown face, he paints the design on to an egg shell, which is then stored in an institute in Paris.

Apr 10

On Good Friday, which is two days before Easter, the Famous Five like to make **Hot Cross Buns**. Here's their recipe:

You will need:
225g self-raising flour
1 teaspoon baking powder
25g castor sugar
50g margarine
100g sultanas
7 tablespoons milk

1. Pre-heat the oven to 220°C (425°F, Gas Mark 7).
2. Pour the flour and baking powder through a sieve into a large bowl, then stir in the castor sugar.
3. Add the margarine, cut into small pieces, and rub the mixture between your fingers until it looks like fine breadcrumbs.
4. Add the sultanas and milk and mix with a metal spoon to turn it into dough.
5. With a rolling-pin and floured board, roll out the dough to a thickness of about 1.5cms.
6. Now use the rim of a glass to cut the dough into circles. Put each one onto a greased baking sheet and, with a sharp knife, cut a cross into the tops of the scones.
7. Place the baking sheet in the middle of the oven for about 12–15 minutes.
8. When the scones are cold, sprinkle icing-sugar into the crosses on the top.

Which of these Easter bunnies is different from all the others?

46

Apr 11

What do you call a rabbit that loses its temper in a heatwave?

Apr 12

A hot cross bun, of course.

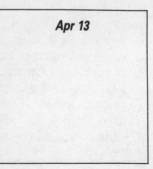

Did someone say 'rabbit'?

On April 12th, 1961, Yuri Gagarin, a Russian cosmonaut, became the first man in space. In his spacecraft, Vostok 1, he remained in orbit for nearly 1½ hours and reached a height of over 300 kilometres above the earth.

Apr 13

There were fears that he might have been violently sick, or battered to bits by meteorites, or killed by radiation. In fact, he was quite unharmed. Some years later, however, he died in an ordinary aircraft crash.

47

Did you know that the first animal in space was a Russian dog? Her name, in English, was Little Lemon!

In 1987, a space-travelling monkey called Yarusha, which means Troublemaker, broke free and horrified all those monitoring the spacecraft's flight by fiddling with the controls!

On the night of March 14th/15th, 1912, the luxury passenger ship *Titanic*, on its first ever voyage, struck an iceberg and sank, causing the loss of 1513 lives. Because of its special design it was thought to be unsinkable, and carried enough lifeboats for only half the passengers.

The Famous Five often go out in George's boat, and they know the rules for **Safety at Sea**. Do you?
1. Always wear a life jacket when sailing or boating.
2. If your boat capsizes, *always stay with it*, even if you can swim. If you get tired, you'll be able to cling to it, and rescuers will be able to see you more easily.
3. If there is nothing to cling to, try not to panic. In

Apr 14

Apr 15

Apr 16

calm water, float on your back. In rough seas, it's best to tread water.
4. Avoid swimming where there are strong currents or tides. If you do have to swim against the current, swim across it diagonally – it's less tiring.
5. Never use an airbed on the sea where there's an off-shore breeze blowing.

By Kirrin Island is the wreck of an old sailing ship that belonged to Henry John Kirrin, one of George's ancestors. In *Five on a Treasure Island*, the Famous Five explore the wreck and find old barrels and cooking pots, bits of furniture and an old wooden box. In the box is a map, which leads to hidden gold!

Apr 17

Have you ever heard of the *Mary Rose*? It was a Tudor warship, the flagship of Henry VIII, which sank in Portsmouth Harbour . in 1545. More than four hundred years later, the wreck was brought to the surface. It's contents were remarkably well preserved and give a vivid picture of life at sea in Tudor times.

Apr 18

In April, the Harness Horse Parade takes place in London's Hyde Park. Can you match these horses with their descriptions?

a. CLYDESDALE **b.** HACKNEY **c.** SUFFOLK PUNCH **d.** COB **e.** SHIRE

1. A thick-set, sturdy type of horse, used for pulling carts or riding.
2. A powerful, heavy breed of carthorse, originally from Scotland.
3. A short-legged, chestnut-coloured breed of draught horse.
4. A compact breed of harness horse with a high-stepping trot.
5. A very large, heavy breed of horse, with long hair on its lower legs, sometimes seen pulling brewers' wagons.

Apr 19

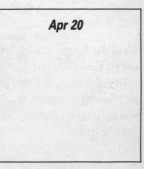

Apr 20

When George gets cross she likes to go off by herself and sulk. There's a type of lightweight horse-drawn vehicle, often used for trotting races in the United States, which is called a sulky – because it can carry only one person.

The Dalmatian dog used to be called the carriage dog. It was trained to run so close behind a carriage that it was between the wheels. This was considered very smart.

Which Dalmatian has the most spots?

People born under the star sign TAURUS (April 21st– May 20th) are lovers of luxury! They prefer a comfortable life, but enjoy outdoor adventures so long as they don't have to get too cold or wet. Famous Taureans include Stevie Wonder, Barbra Streisand and child star Shirley Temple.

Apr 21

What do St George and William Shakespeare have in common? They are both remembered on April 23rd, which is *St George's Day* and also Shakespeare's birthday.

Apr 22

St George is the patron saint of England. Legend tells of his fight with a dragon to rescue a maiden, but in reality he was a Christian martyr who died in Palestine at the time of the Crusades.

Since ancient times, the dragon has represented the power of evil, except in Chinese culture, where the dragon is a kindly monster.

Apr 23

The cross of St George, which was used by Crusaders, is a red cross on a white ground. The Union Flag, or Union Jack, combines St George's cross with the diagonal crosses of St Andrew (for Scotland) and St Patrick (for Ireland).

The Welsh flag shows a red dragon on a green and white background.

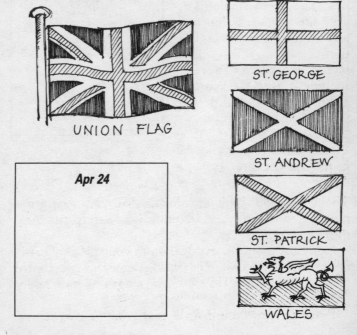

UNION FLAG

ST. GEORGE

ST. ANDREW

Apr 24

ST. PATRICK

WALES

Shakespeare's Birthday Quiz

1. What famous town is associated with William Shakespeare?
2. What was the name of Shakespeare's wife?
3. Which of these is not one of Shakespeare's heroines: Portia, Juliet, Little Nell, Rosalind?
4. What was unusual about the shape of Shakespeare's Globe Theatre?
5. Which of these is a play by Shakespeare: *The Taming of the Lion*, *Edward III*, *A Midsummer's Day's Dream*, *Twelfth Night*?
6. Is Shakespeare known as the Son of Avon, The Bard of Avon or the Scribe of Avon?

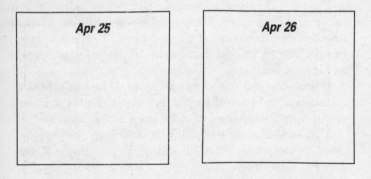

Apr 25

Apr 26

Spin-a-Letter

This is a game to make and play. All you need are a piece of cardboard, a pin and a large safety pin. Any number can play.

Copy the diagram overleaf on to your piece of cardboard. Make the diameter (the distance from the centre to the edge) about 1½ times the length of your safety pin.

Place the cardboard on a magazine or carpet and

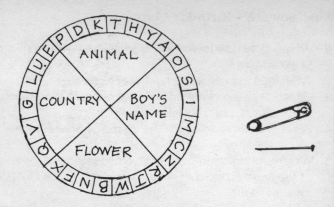

carefully push the pin into the centre. Drop the round end of the safety pin over it. You now have a spinner!

Players take turns to spin the safety pin to find first a subject, then a letter. Suppose the pin lands on Animal on the first spin, and B on the next. The first player must name an animal that begins with the letter B, such as Bear or Badger.

If he succeeds, he scores one point. If he can't think of an answer, and another player *can*, that player scores two points. No answer may be used more than once.

You can change the subjects any time. Some good ones include Articles of Clothing, Pop Groups, Rivers and Famous People.

Apr 27	Apr 28

This picture shows two lines leading from Kirrin Cottage to the beach. What do you think they might represent?

Apr 29

Apr 30

Answers to April puzzles:
Page 46: B is the odd one out. Page 50: 1. d, 2. a, 3. c, 4. b, 5. e, Page 51: The one on the left. Page 53: 1. Stratford-upon-Avon, 2. Anne Hathaway, 3. Little Nell, 4. It was round, 5. 'Twelfth Night', 6. The Bard of Avon. Page 55: The solid line shows the path George might take, and the dotted line is Timmy's, rather longer, route.

MAY

May 1st – *May Day* – is celebrated as a symbol of fertility and growth after the long winter. Until the early 1900s, maypoles decorated with flowers and ribbons were set up in market squares and on village greens. Young men and women danced around the maypole, and the May Queen was crowned with flowers.

May 1

Maypole dancers hold ribbons attached to the top of the pole. As the dancers pass each other, the ribbons weave themselves into patterns. Each dance creates its own particular pattern, and when the ribbons are fully woven, the dancers have to reverse the dance in order to unwind them.

The words 'May Day' are also an international signal for help. In French, '*M'aidez*' means 'Help me', and the radio message 'mayday' means 'I need help urgently'.

May 2

Why not learn the radio alphabet? It's used by all kinds of people, from pilots to policemen, for identifica-

tion. You can use it, too –
when you need to spell out a
name clearly on the tele-
phone, for instance.

A: Alpha B: Bravo
C: Charlie D: Delta
E: Echo F: Foxtrot
G: Golf H: Hotel I: India
J: Juliet K: Kilo L: Lima
M: Mike N: November O: Oscar P: Papa
Q: Quebec R: Romeo S: Sierra T: Tango
U: Uniform V: Victor W: Whisky X: X-ray
Y: Yankee Z: Zulu

Dick's name would be spelt Delta, India, Charlie, Kilo,
and George's Golf, Echo, Oscar, Romeo, Golf, Echo.
How would you spell yours?

The *County Cricket Season*
begins in May with a match
at Lords between the MCC
(Marylebone Cricket Club) and
the previous year's County
Champions. Nobody knows
when the first game of cricket
was played, but the first
formal rules were drawn up in
1740.

Did you know that the
famous cricketer C. B. Fry
once hit a cricket ball into the
fork of a tree? As it could be
seen, and was therefore not a
lost ball, he was able to go on
making runs until the ball was
recovered. In the end he made
sixty-six runs off one ball!

May 6

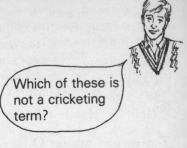

Which of these is not a cricketing term?

YORKER ● BACKWARD POINT ● SLIP ●
SHORT FINE LEG ● HOWZAT ● THIRD MAN ●
SILLY MID OFF ● GOOGLY ● CHINAMAN ●
LEG BREAK ● EXTRA COVER ● LONG ON ●
SQUARE LEG ● GULLY ● HOME RUN ● BUMPER

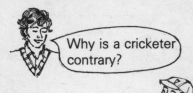

Why is a cricketer contrary?

Because when he's in he goes out, and when he's out he comes in.

May 7

May 8

May 8th is the birthday of Sir David Attenborough, famous for his natural history programmes on television. One of his best-known films shows him sitting among a family of gorillas.

On May 9th, 1671, Colonel Thomas Blood tried to steal the Crown Jewels from the Tower of London. He was caught but not punished, as he had shown up the weaknesses of the security system!

May 9

Tower of London Quiz

1. What birds are associated with the Tower of London?
2. Are the guards at the Tower known as Muffin Men, Beefeaters or Tea Boys?
3. Traitors' Gate leads from the Tower of London to – what?
4. The Tower was used as a prison in World War II. True or false?
5. Among the Crown Jewels are two crowns worn by the Queen – St Edward's crown and the Imperial State crown. Which does she wear for the Opening of Parliament?
6. Which of these was *not* executed in the Tower of London – Katherine Howard, Sir Walter Raleigh, Sir Thomas More, or Mary, Queen of Scots?

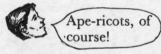

What do baby gorillas sleep in?

Ape-ricots, of course!

59

Ann Boleyn, the second wife of Henry VIII, was beheaded in the Tower of London in May, 1536. She declined the clumsy axe, saying 'I have but a little neck,' and insisted they should send for a special swordsman from France.

The three-day period from May 11th to 13th is known as the *Festival of the Three Ice Men* – St Mamertus, St Pancras and St Servatius. These days are often very cold and frosty.

Here we go gathering nuts in May,
Nuts in May, nuts in May,
Here we go gathering nuts in May,
On a cold and frosty morning.

What's odd about this old rhyme?

May 10

May 11

May 12

There's an old saying about May: 'Ne'er cast a clout (a piece of cloth) till May be out.'

Some people say this means you should wear a vest until the June 1st, but others think 'May' refers to the flowers of the hawthorn, otherwise known as the may tree.

May 13

The hawthorn has white or pink flowers, and later in the year produces fruits called haws.

Try Ann's May Puzzle:

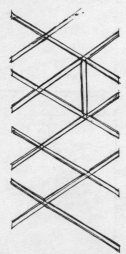

What's this?

May 14

If you are still feeding the birds in your garden, don't put out nuts at this time of year. Baby birds can choke on them!

*A swarm of bees in May
Is worth a load of hay.
A swarm of bees in June
Is worth a silver spoon.
A swarm of bees in July
Is not worth a fly.*

*There once was a man of St
   Bees,
Who was stung on the neck by
   a wasp;
When they asked if it hurt
He replied, 'Not a bit –
It can do it again if it likes!'*

Gardens should be in full leaf by now, so it's an ideal time to play the best of all garden games – **Kick the Can**.

First find an old tin can and a base of some kind. An empty baked bean tin and a big piece of cardboard, for instance. Place the base in the middle of an open space, like a yard or a lawn, and sit the tin can on top of it.

One person is *It*, and must catch all the others.

While *It* stands to one side, one of the other players takes a run at the can and kicks it as far away as possible. Everyone runs and hides while *It* retrieves the can and replaces it on the base. *It* now goes as far from the base as he dares until he sees one of the players. He then shouts, 'Seen you, Julian!' (or whatever

May 15

May 16

May 17

62

the person's name is) and runs back to touch the can. Once *It* has touched the can, Julian is then a prisoner and must stand by the can.

However, if someone else manages to reach the can first and kick it off its base without being caught by *It*, nobody can be caught until the can is put back in place by *It*!

Prisoners (one or several) can be released by one of the other players kicking the can off its base before *It* can catch them. Once everyone has been caught, someone else takes a turn to be *It*.

The best type of garden or park area for *Kick the Can* has an open space surrounded by shrubs or buildings. It is a particularly exciting game if played at dusk.

May 18

Sir Arthur Conan Doyle, creator of the famous detective Sherlock Holmes, was born in May. Like the Famous Five, Sherlock Holmes solved many strange mysteries.

What do you get if you cross a well-known detective with bubble bath?

Sherlock Foams!

May 19

63

Re-arrange these words to give you the names of some famous crime solvers.

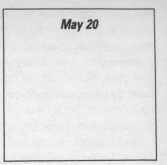

May 20

CURE HER OILPOT
E.A. SHOVE-MUFFIT
REG CABER
SIMMER PALS

Whodunnit?

The residents of a private hotel are shocked to hear that one of the guests has been found dead in the rose garden, stabbed soon after 9 p.m. with an oriental dagger! Among the residents are four suspects, who have all quarrelled with the murder victim. All four claim to have been watching television in their rooms that evening, and make these statements to Inspector L. O. L. Low of the local police.

Mrs Winterbottom: I watched the News on BBC-1. It was about trouble in the Middle East.

Sir Claud Backe: I saw a documentary on BBC-2 about the North Pole. Polar bears and penguins – that sort of thing.

Miss Plimsoll: I was watching a film on ITV. There was a car chase across the Golden Gate Bridge.

May 21

Mr Luckless: I sat through a comedy programme on Channel 4, but I didn't understand the jokes.

Inspector Low made up his mind. 'I am taking one of you in for questioning,' he said. *Which one – and why?*

64

The star sign GEMINI runs from May 21st to June 21st. Gemini is the sign of the twins, and Gemini people are supposed to have two sides to their personalities. They are adventurous and quick, but can be shallow!

Famous Geminians include: Lord Olivier (May 22nd), Joan Collins (May 23rd), Queen Victoria (May 24th) and Clint Eastwood (May 31st).

May 22

The Victoria Cross, or VC, is awarded for 'bravery in the presence of the enemy'. It was instituted in 1856 by Queen Victoria, whose birthday was on May 24th. VCs are cast from the bronze of a cannon captured from the Russians during the Crimean War, and bear the inscription 'For Valour'. The last two VCs were awarded after the Falklands War.

May 23

Animals can be decorated for bravery, too. The RSPCA makes an award called the 'Plaque for Intelligence and Courage', more usually known as the 'Animal VC'. The first one was awarded in the 1950s to a bloodhound named Wolf, who found his way back to his home in Christ-

May 24

church, Dorset, from eighty miles away. More recently an award was made to Hughie, a spaniel cross who rescued his companion Beau after a cliff-top fall.

Timmy could win the Animal VC for some of the things he's done.

Yes – and he's clever too. Timmy – what do two quarters add up to?

Arf!

May 25

May 26

Flapjacks

They're quick and easy to make – and good to take on a half-term picnic!

You will need:
125g porridge oats
100g soft brown sugar
100g hard margarine or butter

1. Preheat the oven to 220°C (425°F, Gas Mark 7).

2. Melt the margarine or butter in a saucepan over moderate heat, then stir in the sugar and oats. Mix well, then spoon the mixture into a shallow baking tin.

3. Press it down firmly, then place the tin in the oven for about 15 minutes.

4. When the mixture is almost cold, cut it into squares with a knife before turning it out.

Try this tongue-twister (but not with a mouth full of flapjack!):

> *Betty bought a bit o' butter*
> *But the butter it was bitter.*
> *So she bought a bit o' better butter*
> *To make the bitter butter better.*

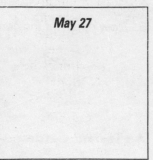

May 27

If you're having a picnic and can't find any paper cups, here's how to make them.

You will need a square of paper about 20cms × 20cms. (Tin foil works, too.)

May 28

1. Fold the paper in half like this

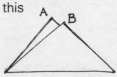

2. Fold C across to D

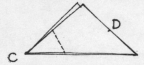

3. Fold E to F

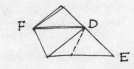

4. Fold down point B towards you, turn the cup over and turn down point A

5. Now open out the centre.

An Instant Garden

At this time of year you can buy plants from garden centres and plant them out. Of course, you can also grow lots of things from seed – cheaper but slower! It's fun to grow things to eat, and if you haven't got a garden you could use a window box, a hanging basket, or even pots on a sunny window-sill. Salad plants like radishes, lettuces, and spring onions are all simple to grow.

Even easier is mustard and cress. You don't need any soil at all for this – just a shallow waterproof container and some kitchen

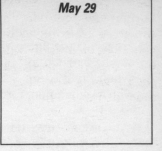

May 29

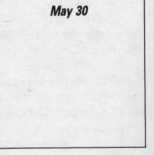

May 30

May 31

68

paper. Put several thicknesses of kitchen paper at the bottom of the container and wet them thoroughly. Sow the cress seeds on to the wet paper, then place the container on a sunny window-sill. Four days later, add the mustard seeds. Right from the start, *make sure the paper is always kept damp*. In a very short time you'll be rewarded with a delicious crop!

Answers to May puzzles:

Page 58: Home run. Page 59: 1. Ravens. 2. Beefeaters. 3. The River Thames. 4. True. 5. The Imperial State crown. 6. Mary, Queen of Scots. Page 60: Nuts don't appear until the autumn, so how can they be picked in May? Page 61: It's the word MAY, on its side. Page 64: Hercule Poirot, The Famous Five, Bergerac, Miss Marple. Page 64: Sir Claude Backe, who was obviously lying. There are no penguins at the North Pole.

JUNE

June 1st was the birthday of Marilyn Monroe. Did you know that her real name was Norma Jean Baker? Here are the real names of some other famous people. Can you say who is who?

1. Marion Morrison
2. Frederick Bulsara
3. David Jones
4. Shirley Crabtree
5. Maurice Micklewhite
6. Priscilla White
7. Reginald Dwight
8. Michael Barratt
9. Marie McDonald
    McLaughlin Lawrie

a. *Cilla Black*
b. *Lulu*
c. *Elton John*
d. *Shakin' Stevens*
e. *John Wayne*
f. *David Bowie*
g. *Big Daddy*
h. *Freddie Mercury*
i. *Michael Caine*

At this time of year the ceremony of *Trooping the Colour* takes place in London. It celebrates Her Majesty the Queen's official birthday,

June 1

June 2

June 3

and comes from the custom of showing a distinctive flag or 'colour' to soldiers before they went into battle, so that they would recognise the flag as a rallying point.

Julian's hints for better cycling

1. Keep your bike in a shed or garage – don't leave it outside.

2. If your bike gets wet, dry it thoroughly before you put it away. This will help to prevent rust.

June 4

3. If you have to leave your bike in the street for a short while, use a padlock and chain to secure it to something that can't move – like railings or a lamppost.

4. Write down the serial number of your bike. (You'll find it engraved somewhere on the frame.) If your bicycle does get stolen, the police will need the number to help trace it.

June 5

5. Keep your tyres pumped

up. The harder they are, the easier it is to pedal.

6. Check your brakes regularly. If they are too weak or too harsh, or if anything on your bike is loose or stiff or buckled, get it seen to. Never ride a bike that isn't in good working order.

7. Don't ride with clothes or bags hanging on the handlebars. These can cause you to lose balance, or they may catch in the front wheel.

June 6

8. Make sure you use front and rear lamps if you go out on your bike after dark. And don't forget to check that they *work*!

9. Always be aware of other road users, and remember that a cyclist is not always easily seen from a car.

10. Read, learn and follow the Highway Code.

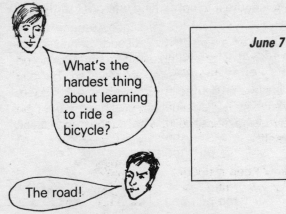

What's the hardest thing about learning to ride a bicycle?

The road!

June 7

If you're interested in bird-watching, you'll know that lots of birds are summer visitors that come here to breed, like cuckoos, swifts, martins and swallows.

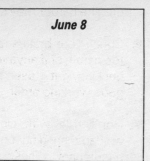
June 8

Have you heard the saying 'One swallow doesn't make a summer'? It means that to see one summer visitor doesn't necessarily mean that summer is here. In other words, don't assume things when you don't have much evidence.

Here's another saying. Do you know which bird it refers to?

June 9

One for sorrow, two for joy,
Three for a girl, four for a
*   boy;*
Five for silver, six for gold,
Seven for a secret that's never
*   been told.*

Secrets have been passed from one person to another in many different ways down the centuries. Genghis Khan, the Mongol ruler who died in 1227, used to send secrets by shaving the heads of his messengers and writing on their bald heads. As the messenger travelled, his hair grew, and after a while the message became hidden. When he reached his destination, his head would be shaved to reveal the message. (It is not suggested that you try this yourself!)

In *Five Go Adventuring Again*, the Famous Five find an old tobacco pouch in a farmhouse . . .

'A few bits of tobacco were still in the pouch – but there was something else, too! Tightly rolled up in the last bit of pouch was a piece of linen. Julian took it out and put it flat on the hall table.

The children stared at it. There were marks and signs on the linen, done in black ink that had hardly faded. But the four of them could not make head or tail of the marks.

"It's not a map," said Julian. "It seems a sort of code, or something. I wish we could make it out. It must be some sort of secret."'

If you found a secret message, would you be able to decipher it? Try these:

HET OLDG IS NI HET DOL
    GWISHIN LWEL

M22T 5S 1T N3N2 5ND2R
    TH2 BR3DG2

OD TON LLET ENOYNA
    TAHW UOY EVAH
    NEES

TFOE NPSF USPPQT

You can send your coded messages to each other by writing them on paper and folding them into darts.

I just caught a code!

June 12

Make your own secret ink by squeezing a little lemon juice into a cup. Dip a nib into it and write your message. To read it, someone will have to hold the paper near something warm, like a radiator.

June 14th is the birthday of Boy George, the famous pop star. Once the lead singer of Culture Club, Boy George now has a successful solo career.

June 13

Around the middle of June comes *Father's Day*. George takes Uncle Quentin his favourite breakfast in bed. He is particularly fond of **Scrambled Egg Faces**:

1. Make toast and scrambled eggs in the usual way, and grill one piece of streaky bacon. (If you're not sure how, get an older person to help you.)

June 14

2. Cut off all four corners of the toast and butter the remainder. Pile on the scrambled eggs.
3. Now make a face on top, using the bacon for a big, smiley mouth, and slices of tomato for the eyes.
4. Use three of the small toast triangles for nose

and eyelids, and eat the last one yourself!

5. If you have any lettuce or parsley, use it for hair.

> **June 15**

> **June 16**

> **June 17**

Cooking outdoors at this time of year is great fun. Apart from the usual hamburgers and pieces of chicken, try some of these:

Sausage Bodgers

Part-cooked sausages sliced down the middle, filled with cheese and wrapped round with bacon spread with chutney. Secure with cocktail sticks and barbecue until the bacon is crisp.

Party Potatoes

Part-cooked jacket potatoes with the insides scooped out, mixed with butter, chopped and cooked onion and bacon, then put the whole thing back together. Wrap tightly in foil and cook until the inside is soft and fluffy.

Tuna Treats

Simply spread tuna and mayonnaise between toast, press down firmly and barbecue until both sides are crisp.

Don't forget that a barbecue fire is *very hot* and small children should be kept away from it. Never use petrol, paraffin, oil or grease to start the fire or to give it a boost, and never leave the fire unattended. A grown-up must always be around.

June 18th is the birthday of ex-Beatle Paul McCartney. The Beatles were known as 'The Fab Four'. There are ten Beatles song titles hidden in this story. Can you find them?

June 18

The Famous Five and the Fab Four

It was the first day of the holidays. Anne and George came down to breakfast.

'Good morning, good morning,' they said to the boys.

'It's a lovely day,' added Anne. 'Look – here comes the sun!'

'What shall we do today?' said Dick. He thought a walk down Penny Lane to visit Eleanor Rigby would be fun.

'I saw a yellow submarine near Kirrin Island,' said Julian. 'We should take the long and winding road over the cliffs to look at it. I've got a feeling it's up to no good.'

'Let's ask Aunt Fanny,' suggested Anne. 'Your mother should know what it's doing there,' she said to George.

With Timmy at their heels, they all trooped into the kitchen.

'The submarine?' said Aunt Fanny. 'Oh, that's just on a magical mystery tour. I should let it be if I were you.'

Cherries should be ripening now. Count the stones on your plate to find out your fate.

Who will I marry? Tinker, tailor, soldier, sailor, rich man, poor man, beggarman, thief.

What will I drive to church in? Coach, carriage, wheelbarrow, donkey cart.

What will I wear? Silk, satin, cotton, rags.

What will I live in? Big house, little house, pigsty, barn.

How many children will I have? 1, 2, 3, 4, etc.

> **June 19**

If you were born between June 22nd and July 22nd, you come under the star sign CANCER (the crab). Cancer people tend to be restless, never happy to stay in one place for long. When adventure beckons – they're off!

Famous Cancerians include Yul Brynner, Ringo Starr and Noel Edmonds.

> **June 20**

> **June 21**

June 22

The rocky pools left on Kirrin Island when the tide goes out are good places to look for crabs. Their shells, or carapaces, are jointed, like suits of armour. As the animal inside grows, its shell splits off and is replaced by a new, larger one.

June 22nd is the Longest Day – the midsummer solstice.

Here's a good game to play outdoors:

June 23

Turtle Race

Any number can play. It's a bit like a three-legged race, except that four people are all tied together.

Each team of four people needs a length of rope. The four stand back to back and are tied together around their waists. Teams line up to start.

On the word 'Go', the turtle-teams have to move as quickly as possible towards the finishing line, about 30 metres away. If they fall over, or 'turn turtle', they may have quite a struggle to get upright again. First over the line wins the race!

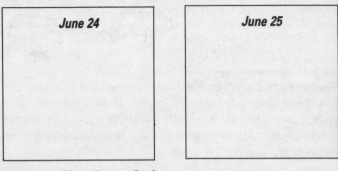

| June 24 | June 25 |

Famous Five June Quiz

How well do you know the Famous Five stories?

1. How many books are there in the Famous Five series? 21
2. In *Five Go Adventuring Again*, what is the name of the tutor?
3. What does Timmy love to chase? rabbits
4. In *Five Run Away Together*, where does Julian first find Mr Stick?
5. In *Five on a Treasure Island*, what is inside the old box rescued from the wreck?
6. What is Pierre Lenoir's nickname, in *Five Go to Smuggler's Top*? sooty
7. In *Five Fall into Adventure*, where do Aunt Fanny and Uncle Quentin go on holiday?
8. In which book are Maggie and Dirty Dick looking for stolen jewels?
9. In *Five on Kirrin Island Again*, who goes to live on the island?

10. Who accompanies the Famous Five in *Five Go Off to Camp*?

I SAY I SAY

WHY DID YOU SAY I SAY I SAY

I SAY I SAY I DIDN'T SAY I SAY I SAY

I SAY I SAID I SAY I SAY SEE I SAY I SAY I SAY I SAY NOT I SAY I SAY YOU SEE

IF YOU SAY SO NOW TELL ME THE JOKE

I'VE FORGOTTEN IT!

(*Could you make sense of all that?*)

June 26	June 27

The last week in June sees the start of the *All-England Lawn Tennis Championships* at Wimbledon.

Lawn tennis has its origins in a game played by the ancient Persians and Egyptians. Centuries later, French noblemen played *jeu de paume*, in which they used their hands to hit a ball over a net. From this came the game of Real Tennis, also called Court or Royal Tennis – a game that is still played today.

In 1874 a Major Wingfield invented 'a portable court for playing the ancient game of tennis', and the idea caught on. Three years later, the first lawn tennis championship was held.

June 28

June 29

June 30

Answers to June puzzles:

Page 70: 1. e., 2. h., 3. f., 4. g., 5. i., 6. a., 7. c., 8. d., 9. b.
Page 73: Magpie. Page 74: 1. The gold is in the old wishing well. 2. Meet me at nine under the bridge. (The vowels A, E, I, O, U are replaced by 1, 2, 3, 4, 5.) 3. Do not tell anyone what you have seen. 4. Send more troops. (Each letter is represented by the one that comes after it in the alphabet.) Page 77: 'Good Morning, Good Morning', 'Here Comes the Sun', 'Penny Lane', 'Eleanor Rigby', 'Yellow Submarine', 'The Long and Winding Road', 'I've Got a Feeling', 'Your Mother Should Know', 'Magical Mystery Tour', 'Let It Be'. Page 80: 1. 21. 2. Mr Roland. 3. Rabbits. 4. Asleep on a sofa in the kitchen. 5. A map of Kirrin Castle. 6. Sooty. 7. Spain. 8. 'Five on a Hike Together'. 9. Uncle Quentin. 10. Mr Luffy, the schoolmaster. Page 81: Dick: I say, I say! Anne: Why did you say, 'I say I say I say'? Dick: I say I didn't say 'I say, I say, I say'. I said 'I say, I say.' See? Anne: I say 'I say I say I say,' not 'I say I say,' you see.

JULY

July 1st is the birthday of the Princess of Wales. As Lady Diana Spencer, she married Prince Charles on July 29th, 1981, in St Paul's Cathedral. She wore an ivory-coloured fairytale dress, with big, puffed sleeves, and was attended by 5 bridesmaids and 2 pageboys. Her going-away outfit was coral pink silk, with an ostrich-feather hat.

July 1

Other well-known people born in July include Dr David Owen (2nd), Ringo Starr (7th), David Essex (23rd), Mick Jagger (26th), and Daley Thompson (30th).

The so-called 'dog days' start around now. They are supposed to be the hottest time of the year and are called 'dog days' because they coincide with the rising of Sirius, the Dog Star (the brightest star in the sky).

July 2

Are you Sirius?

On July 4th, 1845, Thomas John Barnardo was born in Ireland. He went to London to study medicine, then, at the age of 25, opened his first Home for Destitute Boys, in Stepney. Three years later came a Home for Girls, at Barkingside. There are now over a hundred Dr Barnardo's Homes in the UK, and several overseas. Their motto is 'No destitute child ever refused admission'.

July 3

July 4

July 5

July is a good month for observing clouds, as they can often be seen against a bright blue sky. See if you can spot any of these and use them to predict the weather:

Stratus (horizontal, low clouds) – there may be drizzle about.

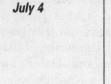

Cumulus (rounded heaps of cloud) – fine weather cloud.

Cirrus (high, curling clouds, sometimes called 'mares' tails') – rain is on the way.

85

Also watch out for:
Cumulo-nimbus (towering fluffy clouds, dark underneath) – heavy showers and thunderstorms.
Cirro-cumulus (a 'mackerel' sky) – 'never long wet and never long dry'.
Nimbo-stratus (dark, flat, low cloud) – prolonged rain.

July 6

July 7

July gets its name from the Roman emperor Julius Caesar. His birthday was July 12th. Julian's name comes from the same source, and the names of the other members of the Famous Five have meanings, too:

Dick (Richard) means 'hard ruler'
Anne means 'graceful'
George means 'farmer'
Timmy (Timothy) means 'honouring God'

July 8

July 9

See if you can find out the meaning of your own name. If you can also discover on which day of the week you were born, you can use this poem to see what type of person you're supposed to be.

Monday's child is fair of face;
Tuesday's child is full of
grace;
Wednesday's child is full of
woe;
Thursdays child has far to go;
Friday's child is loving and
giving;
Saturday's child works hard for
a living;
But the child that is born on
the Sabbath day
Is bonny and blithe and good
and gay.

Uncle Quentin knows a great way to make a barometer. It's really easy, and will show you when changes in atmospheric pressure are taking place – a good way to know what's happening to the weather.

You need a long-necked, clear glass bottle and a clear glass jar (or drinking glass) that will fit snugly over it, with the

July 13

July 14

mouth of the bottle just clear of the base of the jar.

Colour some water with ink or food colouring, then pour a little into the bottle. Now invert the jar over the bottle, then, holding them tightly together, quickly turn them up the other way. Most of the water will run into the jar, but some will stay in the neck of the bottle. You may need to experiment a little, to get the right amount of water.

When the water in the bottle rises, the weather is going to be fine. When it falls, take your umbrella!

It really works!

The rain it raineth on the just
And also on the unjust fella,
But chiefly on the just, because
The unjust steals the just's
umbrella.

(Charles, Baron Bowen)

July 15th is *St Swithin's Day*. St Swithin was made Bishop of Winchester in the year 852, and legend has it that the weather conditions on St Swithin's Day will continue for the next forty days.

July 15

Did you know that although in England it may rain 'cats and dogs', in France it rains 'small spears', and in Germany 'bits of string'!

This sentence helps to remind us of the colours in a rainbow: *Richard of York Gravely Battled in Vain.*
Can you name them?

If the weather is hot there might be a thunderstorm. They say that if you count slowly between a lightning flash and the roll of thunder that follows it, the number tells you roughly how many miles away the storm is happening.

Do you know what to do if you're caught outdoors in a thunderstorm? *Don't* shelter under a tall, isolated tree, or in the mouth of a cave. Both of these may attract lightning.

If you're in the middle of an open field, lie flat on your stomach. The lightning is looking for the tallest thing around to conduct it down to the earth, so you need to make sure you're well clear of anything that might attract it. You should be reasonably safe in a wood, where all the trees are roughly the

July 16

July 17

July 18

same height, or you can shelter in a hollow in the ground, or in a car. (A car makes a bad lightning conductor because its rubber tyres prevent the electricity from reaching the ground.)

Aunt Fanny's Pot-Pourri

For this long-lasting mixture of fragrant petals, you will need:

July 19

Pretty china containers
Petals from sweet-smelling flowers, such as roses, lavender, stock, rosemary, thyme and honeysuckle
Mint and bay leaves
125g each of common salt, brown sugar and coarse salt
15g each of cinnamon, ground cloves, nutmeg and borax
Wire cake racks
A large, airtight jar

Dry the petals and leaves on the cake racks in an airing cupboard for 2–3 weeks. Mix the other ingredients together and pour them into the jar in alternate layers with the dried petals and leaves. Close the jar and wait three days, then mix everything well together. For the next three weeks, stir the mixture regularly, then pour it into china pots or bowls and place it around the house. It will make all the rooms smell lovely (despite the fact that the name *pot-pourri* – pronounced po-poo-ree – is the French for 'rotten pot'!).

On July 20th, 1969, man first set foot on the moon. As Apollo XI spacecraft commander Neil Armstrong stepped out of the landing module, he said, 'That's one small step for a man – one giant leap for mankind.'

July 20	July 21

Would you like some green cheese?

No thanks, I'm full.

July 22 — got this Diary.

If the weather looks fine, the Famous Five often decide to take a picnic to the beach. Here's a **sandwich recipe** they all enjoy:

1. Cut a crusty roll in half and scoop out most of the bottom half and some of the top half.

2. Fill the bottom half with any mixture you like, piling it high, then put the top on. You might like to try some of these fillings:

91

- ★ Hard-boiled eggs and tomatoes in mayonnaise
- ★ Cold sausages and baked beans
- ★ Cubes of cheddar cheese mixed with pickle

3. Wrap the roll tightly in foil or cling film to keep it fresh.

People born between July 23rd and August 23rd come under the star sign LEO. They are go-getters, who like to push ahead with things, and some of them like to think themselves a little superior to others.

Famous Leos include Mick Jagger, Terry Wogan and Steve Davis.

July 23

The word 'leo' means lion. Can you identify these names, which all contain LEO?

1. Another name for a panther.
2. A queen of ancient Egypt.
3. A lizard that changes colour.
4. He painted the *Mona Lisa*.
5. A large sailing vessel.
6. Something worn by dancers and gymnasts.

July 24

92

It's holiday time, and if you're going on a long journey by car, here's a game to help pass the time:

July 25

Ten Past

Watch the cars going the opposite way to you. If the road has several traffic lanes on each side, choose the one nearest (such as the fast lane of a motorway). Everyone (except the driver, of course!) has to guess the make and colour of the tenth car to pass you. Two points for the right colour, five for the right make, and twenty points if you guess both colour and make correctly! Play as quietly as you can so as not to distract the driver.

Knock Knock!

Who's there?

Tim.

Tim who?

Timpossible to say!

July 26

July 27

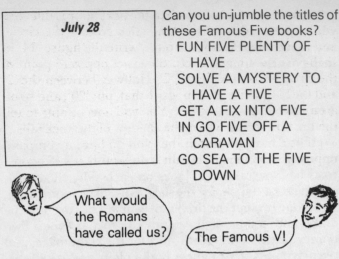

July 28

Can you un-jumble the titles of these Famous Five books?

FUN FIVE PLENTY OF HAVE

SOLVE A MYSTERY TO HAVE A FIVE

GET A FIX INTO FIVE

IN GO FIVE OFF A CARAVAN

GO SEA TO THE FIVE DOWN

What would the Romans have called us?

The Famous V!

Make a Beach Sundial

All you need are a long, thin stick, 50cms of string, a small, sharp stick and some small shells or pebbles.

Plant the long stick in a smooth, flat piece of sand. Tie a loop in each end of the string. Place one loop over the long stick, so that it rests on the ground, and hold the short stick in the other loop. Keeping the string taut, draw a circle in the sand by walking round, scratching the sand with the short stick. Remove the string and short stick.

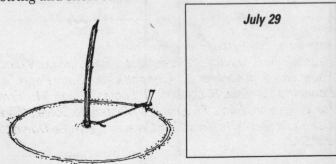

July 29

94

Look at a watch to see when the next hour is due. See where the shadow of the long stick crosses the circle, and make a mark. If it's 2 p.m., write the figure '14' in shells over your mark. On the exact opposite point of the circle, make the figure '2'. Halfway between the '2' and the '14', write '8'. Opposite that, put '20', and so on around your 24-hour clock. You will now be able to tell the time by seeing where the shadow of the stick falls.

(If you have no watch, but you do have a compass, remember that when the sun is due south, it's 12 noon.)

July 30

camping!

July 31

Deliphias
birthday

Answers to July Puzzles:
Page 89: Red, Orange, Yellow, Green, Blue, Indigo, Violet.
Page 92: 1. Leopard. 2. Cleopatra. 3. Chameleon. 4. Leonardo da Vinci. 5. Galleon. 6. Leotard. Page 94: 'Five Have Plenty of Fun', 'Five Have a Mystery to Solve', 'Five Get Into a Fix', 'Five Go off in a Caravan', 'Five Go Down to the Sea'.

AUGUST

August 1st used to be called *Lammas (Loaf-Mass) Day*, and was a day of thanksgiving for the first corn harvested.

Here are four kinds of corn – *Barley*, *Wheat*, *Oats* and *Maize*. Do you know which is which?

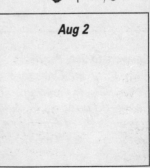
Aug 1

A   B   C   D

Barley is used in making beer and whisky, and is a nourishing food for cattle and pigs. It's also milled to produce pearl and pot barley (used in soups and stews).

Aug 2

Wheat is turned into flour for making bread, cakes, pastry and biscuits. Toasted flakes of wheat make popular breakfast cereals. Hard, or durum, wheat is used for pasta and semolina, and wheat straw (the stalks) can be used for thatching and as a bedding for livestock.

Oats and oatstraw are used as feed and bedding for animals, and oatmeal (ground-up oats) is made into porridge and oatcakes.

Aug 3

Maize is often eaten as a vegetable (corn on the cob or sweetcorn), and as a breakfast cereal. It's made into flour, too. Maize is a good food for animals, and oil can be extracted from it.

Famous August birthdays include The Princess Royal (15th), Robert Redford (18th), Princess Margaret (21st) and Geoff Capes (23rd). To read about someone extra-special who was born in August, turn to August 11th!

Aug 4

Cowes Week

Cowes is a pretty little port on the Isle of Wight, best known for its world-famous yachting centre. At this time of year, a week-long sailing regatta takes place at Cowes.

 What do people in Cowes eat for breakfast?

 Moo-sli, I expect!

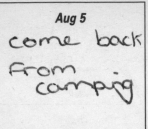

Aug 5

come back
from
camping

Can you identify all these parts of a sailing boat?
TRANSOM, TILLER, GAFF, BURGEE, SPINNAKER, KEEL, BOOM, BATTEN, JIB, FORESTAY, RUDDER.

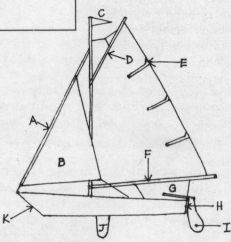

When ships want to communicate with each other, or with the land, they often use some kind of signalling.

Before the invention of radio telegraphy, one of the ways vessels talked to each other was by flag signals. Every ship has its own identifying 'name', consisting of

Aug 6

four signal letters, and flags are hoisted singly, or in groups of two, three or four. Every letter of the alphabet has its own flag, which sometimes has its own meaning, too.

98

For instance O also means 'Man Overboard', 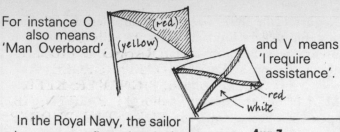 and V means 'I require assistance'.

In the Royal Navy, the sailor who sets up flag signals is known as a bunting tosser. Sometimes flags are used when radio silence has to be maintained – for instance, if an enemy might be listening in.

Aug 7

Another way to signal with flags is to use semaphore. To send messages by semaphore, you hold a flag in each hand and indicate letters by moving the positions of your arms. Even if you don't understand semaphore, perhaps you can understand whose name is being spelt out here. (Clue: It's one of the Famous Five!)

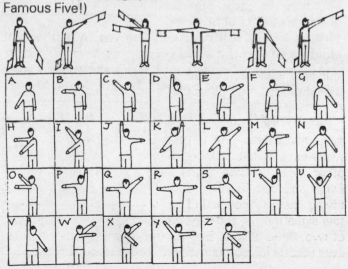

August 11th, 1897, was the day on which Enid Mary Blyton was born in a flat above a shop at East Dulwich, in South London. Most of her childhood was spent in Beckenham, and after she left school she trained to be a teacher. Around this time she had several poems published, and when she was 23 she sold a fairy story to a magazine.

> **Aug 8**
>
> hoannes birthday! (my best friend).

This was the beginning of an amazing career. Before Enid Blyton died, at the age of 71, she had written over 600 books, together with numerous songs, poems and plays. She ran clubs and magazines for her readers and was the most popular children's writer of her time.

> **Aug 9**

Her books are still read and enjoyed by millions of children all over the world.

Among the characters and series she created were The Famous Five (of course!), Noddy, Mary Mouse,

> **Aug 10**

> **Aug 11**
>
> Ninas birthday

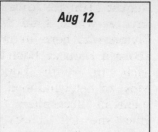

Aug 12

Malory Towers, The Secret Seven, the Circus books and the Adventure and Mystery books. She loved nature and often wrote about the countryside around Green Hedges – the house in Beaconsfield, Bucks, where she lived with her first husband, Hugh Pollock (the father of her two daughters, Gillian and Imogen), and, later, with her second husband, Kenneth Darrell Waters.

Her last book, published in 1968, was called *Once Upon a Time*.

The Enid Blyton Trust for Children

Aug 13

Please think for a moment about those children who are unable to do the exciting things most children can do – perhaps because they are sick or handicapped. One of the projects sponsored by the Trust is the National Library for the Handicapped Child (the Blyton Handi-Read Centre), which provides books for children with special needs.

Would you like to help the Trust by making a small donation? If so, send a postal order to The Enid Blyton Trust for Children, Third Floor, New South Wales House, 15 Adam Street, London WC2N 6AH. Thank you.

Aug 14	Aug 15

Blyton Quiz

1. Who is Noddy's best friend? big ears
2. Enid Blyton wrote 'The Naughtiest Girl is a —' what? monitor
3. What are the names of the twins at St Clare's? Pat an Isbel
4. In which Blyton series does a boy have a pet parrot? mystrey
5. Which school series features a girl called Darrell Rivers? mabry towers

Aug 16	Aug 17

6. What are Barbara, Colin, Janet, Peter, George, Pam and Jack known as? *secret seven*

7. In *The Rockingdown Mystery* what type of animal is Loony? *a dog*

8. How many Find-Outers did Enid Blyton write about? *15*

9. What type of entertainment does Mr Galliano provide? *a circus*

10. What grows out of the legs of the Wishing Chair?

11. In which wood is the magic Faraway Tree?

12. Are Binkle and Flip goblins, squirrels, twin boys, rabbits or clowns? *rabbits*

Would you like to join the Famous Five Club and wear the Famous Five badge? There are friends of the Famous Five all over the world – wear your badge and you'll know each other at once! To join the club, just send a 20p postal order or postage stamp (no coins please), with a stamped envelope addressed to yourself, inside an envelope addressed to: FAMOUS FIVE CLUB, c/o Darrell Waters Ltd, 3rd Floor, New South Wales House, 15 Adam Street, London WC2N 6AH.

The Famous Five often camp out on Kirrin Island during their adventures, and they know how important it is to choose the right place for pitching their tent:

1. Find a site near a clear stream, if you can. You can use the water for washing and drinking.

Aug 18
my birthday

Before drinking stream water, boil it first for five minutes, or use water-purifying tablets.

Aug 19
go to France!

2. Pick a spot that's dry and level – no stones, lumps or thistles! Avoid anywhere that's likely to be flooded in a rainstorm.
3. Keep away from places that attract insects, and avoid long grass, which is likely to be damp.
4. Don't camp under trees. A strong wind could bring down branches, and the leaves will continue to drip long after a shower has passed. Also, of course, a tall, isolated tree may attract lightning.
5. Before you pitch your tent, remember that you must ask permission from the landowner first. (George is the owner of Kirrin Island, so she just has to ask herself!) If you want to make a camp fire, you should ask about that, too.

Aug 20

If the weather looks fine, you can shelter in an open-ended tent, which is quite easy to make. All you need are a large, heavy-duty sheet of polythene, two stout poles (preferably pointed at one end), four lengths of thick string or rope, and ten 15cm nails.

First, drive the poles firmly into the ground so that they stand upright. The distance between them should be the width of the sheet. Fold the sheet in half width-ways and nail the middle edge of the sheet to the top of one of the poles, then tie two guy ropes to the nail. Make loops at the ends of the guy ropes and nail

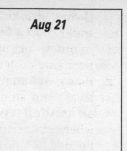
Aug 21

them into the ground, with the nails at a steep angle away from the tent. Now nail the sheet to the second pole and fix the other two ropes in the same way. You will probably need to reposition the guy ropes to make the tent firm and steady. Fold up the edges of the sheet and use the remaining four nails to pin them to the ground.

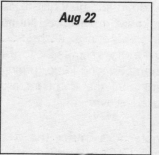
Aug 22

If you have permission to light a camp fire, remember that fires can easily get out of control and set light to large areas of heath or woodland, so *be very careful where you build it.*

Collect some kindling (small sticks and bits of wood), some tinder (feathers, dry grass, tree bark etc.), and some small logs.

Enclose the tinder in a triangle of sticks. Light the tinder, then add kindling so that a cone is formed.

When the fire is well alight, add logs in a star

shape. As the logs burn at one end, just push them further into the centre.

Before you leave a camp fire, *always* make sure it is completely out by throwing sand or earth on top of it.

Aug 23

Here's an easy camp fire recipe:

Dampers

Mix together some flour and a pinch of salt. Add water slowly to make a stiff dough (not too wet). Use a sharp knife to peel the bark off some long sticks, then twist a lump of dough round one end of each stick. Lay the sticks across the top of the embers and keep turning them until the dampers are cooked all over.

Fill them with butter and jam. Mmm – lovely!

Aug 24

People born under the star sign VIRGO (August 24th–September 23rd) are supposed to be shy and reserved, but they often hide their true natures!

Famous Virgoans include Russ Abbot, Sophia Loren and Michael Jackson.

106

Campers often like to go hiking. It's just another name for walking, really, and a hike may last just a few hours or perhaps several days.

Wear a strong and comfortable pair of shoes or boots and take a cagoule or anorak in case of bad weather. It helps to carry a compass and a map of the area in which you're walking.

How good are you at map reading? Here's Dick walking through Kirrin Village. If he follows these directions, where does he end up?

Turn left at the T-junction. Take the south-east fork. Turn right before the railway bridge. After the church with a spire, turn left. Take the road that goes round the marsh and turn left before the pub. When you reach some houses, turn left again. At the crossroads go south, and it's on your right.

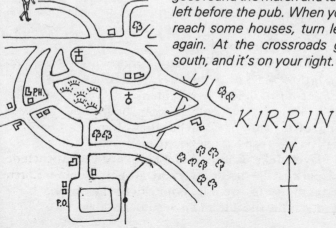

KIRRIN

Aug 27	Aug 28

Aug 29

Aug 30

August is a month for outdoor fun, but if there's a rainy day, try this card game. The Famous Five love playing cards, and this one is called **Fivesies**:

Use an ordinary pack of playing cards. Shuffle it, and deal five cards to each player. Place the rest of the pack face down in the centre and turn the top card over to start a discard pile. Each player places his or her cards face up on the table.

The object of the game is to obtain either three of a kind (three sixes, three jacks, etc.) or a run of four (e.g. 5, 6, 7, 8 or 10, jack, queen, king) of any suit. Aces can be high or low (used as one or to follow a king).

Players take turns first to pick a card from the top of the pack or the discard pile, then to discard a card face up on to the discard pile. When all the cards have been used, shuffle the pile and place it face down, as before.

108

The winner is the first player to collect three of a kind or complete a run.

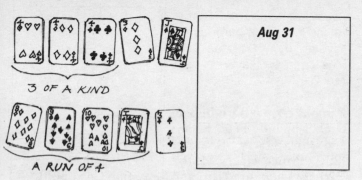

3 OF A KIND

A RUN OF +

Aug 31

SEPTEMBER

According to the old Roman calendar, September was the seventh month of the year. (The Latin for seven is *septem*.)

Sept 1

Famous people born in September include Peter Sellers and Sir Harry Secombe (8th), Prince Harry (15th), Barbara Dickson (27th) and Sebastian Coe (29th).

Prince Harry's real name is Henry, which used to be a very popular name for royal boys – England has had eight King Henrys!

Here's a rhyme to help you remember the Kings and Queens of England from William the Conqueror to Elizabeth II.

Sept 2

Willy, Willy, Harry, Stee,
Henry, Dick, John, Harry 3;
1 2 3 Teds, then Dick 2,
Henry 4 5 6, then who?
Edward 4, 5, Dick the Bad,
Henry, Henry, Ted the
   Lad;
Mary, Elizabeth, James
   the Vain,
Charlie, Charlie, James again;
William and Mary, then Queen Anne,
Georges four and Willi-am;
Vicky, Ted, George, Edward 8
(the only king to abdicate);
George the Sixth, then Lizzie 2
(Our present queen) – and now we're through.

It's the end of the summer holidays, and time to be thinking about school again. Here's a puzzle to get you back into practice. (Clue: Your answers should add up to 100.)

How many . . .

dwarfs befriended Snow White?

events made up a pentathlon?

players are there in a rugby union team?

blackbirds were 'baked in a pie'?

millimetres in a centimetre?

lives is a cat said to have?

wives had Henry VIII?

'lords a-leaping' in the Christmas song?

riders on a tandem?

noughts in ten million?

players in a quintet?

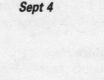

Sept 3

Sept 4

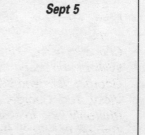

Sept 5

....

....

....

....

....

....

There was an old man who said, 'Do
Tell me how I should add two and two?
I think more and more
That it makes about four –
But I fear that is almost too few.'

Julian, will you help me with my maths homework?

Certainly not! It wouldn't be right.

Maybe not, but you could at least try!

Everybody should know the basic rules of **First Aid**. To learn what to do in an emergency, and be of real help to people – perhaps even saving their lives – you should join the Red Cross or St John Ambulance Brigade, both of which have junior sections. Cubs, Brownies, Scouts and Guides also give a very good basic training in First Aid.

For minor problems, remember these simple rules:

Small cuts and grazes: Bathe the wound and cover it with a clean dressing.

Sept 6

Sept 7

Sept 8

112

Sept 9

Burns: Cool the affected area (perhaps by holding it under a cold tap), dry gently and cover with a clean dressing.

Bee stings: Pull out the sting with tweezers, then bathe the area with bicarbonate of soda dissolved in water.

Wasp stings: Bathe with vinegar or lemon juice.

Speck in the eye: Roll the eyelid back and try gently to flick out the dirt with a cotton bud or the corner of a clean handkerchief. If this doesn't work, get the patient to blink his eye in a basin of cool water.

Sept 10

Nosebleed: Tell the patient to pinch the bridge of his nose firmly.

Feeling faint: Lie the patient down with his feet higher than his head, or get him to sit with his head hanging down between his knees.

Sept 11

If you are ever at the scene of a serious accident, the first thing you should do is to *summon expert help*. Either telephone for an ambulance yourself, or ask someone else to do it. While you're waiting for an ambulance to arrive,

DO comfort the patient and keep him warm.

113

DON'T move him or give him anything to eat or drink.

And remember: if you're not sure what kind of first aid to give, do nothing. Doing the wrong thing can sometimes make matters worse.

The one first aid skill that everybody should learn is how to give mouth-to-mouth resuscitation. It can save the life of a person who has ceased to breathe as a result of an accident or heart attack. Try to find a class where you can practise this technique on special dummies. One day, you may use it to save someone's life.

What's happened to the mistletoe berries you planted in April, George?

Look – the mistletoe plants are beginning to grow. Will we have berries this Christmas?

I'm afraid not. You have to wait two or three years for the plants to become mature. But after that, there should be berries galore!

Do you know what *TRIS-KAIDEKAPHOBIA* means? It's an overwhelming fear of the number 13! People with this strange phobia daren't go out on the 13th of the month in case something terrible happens to them.

114

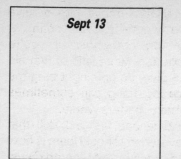

Sept 13

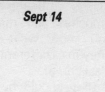

Sept 14

Sept 15

It's said that September 15th is nearly always a fine day in England. It's *Battle of Britain Day*, when we commemorate the big air battle of World War II. It was actually a series of battles over London and South-East England between the Royal Air Force and the German Luftwaffe, which took place between August and October, 1940. Victory for the RAF put an end to the threat of Germany invading the British Isles. Sir Winston Churchill said: 'Never in the field of human conflict was so much owed by so many to so few.'

Battle of Britain pilots came to be known as 'The Few'.

Sept 16

Blaggs, brammel kites, mooches and mushes! Do you know what they are? They're all different names for blackberries.

They should be ready for picking now, so here's Anne's special recipe for **Blackberry Yoghurt**:

Sept 17

1. Put some blackberries in a saucepan with some sugar (about two teaspoons of sugar to each large handful of blackberries).

Sept 18

2. Heat the pan until the blackberries are mushy and the sugar has dissolved.
3. Let the blackberries cool a little, then push them through a sieve into a basin. The pips should stay behind in the sieve.
4. Add the strained blackberries to plain yoghurt for a deliciously different dessert.

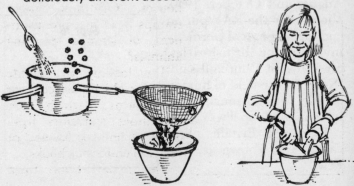

116

Timmy, the top of a house is called the . . .

Woof!

Correct. Now tell me the name of a night-bird.

H-o-owl!

Good. Now, what does R-A-B-B-I-T spell?

Timmy . . . ?
Timmy . . . ?

Sept 19

Sept 20

Do you enjoy collecting things? It's possible to make an interesting collection of almost anything.

The most exciting and unusual collections are usually those that centre on some particular theme. For instance, not just postcards, but postcards showing lighthouses. Or how about stamps from just one continent, or stamps featuring animals?

Try looking in jumble sales for old model cars, or snowstorms (which are sometimes souvenirs from different holiday towns), or very old children's books.

To make your own

117

museum, look around gardens for interesting scraps of glass and china. Near old houses one can sometimes find pieces of clay pipes, horseshoes and old bottles with glass stoppers. If you're very lucky, you might even find an old coin or a fossil or a flint axe-head. But even a strangely-shaped stone or piece of driftwood can make an interesting exhibit.

You can build display shelves by glueing boxes together. Cover them with paper first, or paint the whole assembly when the glue is dry.

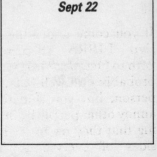

Sept 21

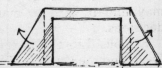

Sept 22

The football season is well under way now. If you'd like to play football without getting cold, try this version:

Blow Football

Make the goals by cutting out two pieces of card as shown, then bending back the sides.

Stick these to a table with sticky tape. (Ask permission first, and don't *ever* stick anything to a polished table!) Place books around the edge of the table to form a barrier.

All you need now is a drinking straw for each player, and a ping pong ball.

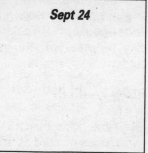

If you come under the star sign LIBRA (September 24th to October 23rd) you're probably a well-balanced person, but you sometimes annoy other people by insisting that they try to see both sides of everything! You may find it hard to make decisions.

Famous Librans include George Peppard, Steve Ovett and the Duchess of York.

Libra Puzzle

These sentences all point to a word which describes the symbol for Libra. What is it?
1. Fish have them.
2. The window cleaner
   _ _ _ _ _ _ a ladder.
3. Groups of notes in ascending or descending order.
4. Removes a deposit left by hard water.
5. Used for weighing.

Believe It or Not

Language changes over the years, and English people of long ago used to count like this:

Ane, tane, tother, feather, flip,
Sother, lother, co, deffrey, dick,
Een dick, teen dick, tother dick, feather dick, bumfrey,
Een bumfrey, teen bumfrey, tother bumfrey, feather bumfrey,
gigot (twenty).

If I had feather apples in one hand, and bumfrey in the other, what would I have?

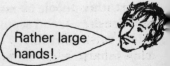

Rather large hands!

120

Have you got a cat? Do you take good care of it? Cats are not as independent as people often think, and they'll repay care and consideration given to them with years of companionship and affection.

A cat will sleep almost anywhere, but will appreciate a box or blanket in a warm place, lined with something cosy. Remember to wash the bedding regularly.

Try to give your cat a balanced diet – most tinned foods contain all a cat needs – and make sure he always has water to drink (even if he has milk as well). Keep his bowls clean, but wash them separately from the family's dishes.

Grooming removes loose hair, parasites (such as fleas!) and dirt. It's especially important for long-haired cats. Gently comb the fur with a fine comb then, for an extra-smart coat, finish off with a soft brush.

All cats need to keep their claws sharp. They do this by scratching them on anything convenient – often the furniture! Provide your cat with a scratching post: a piece of wood, such as a log, covered with an old bit of carpet or other tough material. Your furniture should then be safe.

A popular myth about cats is they like to be put out at night. Nothing could be further from the truth. A cat likes to be in a warm, comfortable bed at night, just like you! Let your cat out for a short time in the evening, but make sure he's safely indoors at night.

Sept 30

Answers to September puzzles:
Page 111: 7, 5, 15, 24, 10, 9, 6, 10, 2, 7, 5. Page 120: Scales.

OCTOBER

Oct 1

The Slavs call October the 'yellow month', because of the falling leaves. An old German name for it means 'wine month'. In England it has long been the main month for brewing.

Brewing Your Own Ginger Beer

Oct 2

The Famous Five like to brew their own ginger beer. Here's their recipe. If you start now, you'll have lots of ginger beer to drink at Christmas!

You will need:
25g dried yeast
ground ginger
2 lemons
About 1kg sugar

Oct 3

1. Take 300ml of tepid water, 1 teaspoonful of sugar and the yeast and mix them thoroughly in a large coffee jar.
2. Every day for the next 7 days stir in ½ teaspoonful of ground ginger and 1

teaspoonful of sugar. Make sure that you use a wooden spoon for stirring – yeast hates metal! In between stirring, keep your jar upright and still and keep it covered with a piece of kitchen paper.

Oct 4

3. Next strain the liquid from the solid mass at the bottom of the jar – DO NOT THROW THE SOLID MATERIAL AWAY! Use a nylon sieve for straining, not a metal one. This must be done very thoroughly as no solid matter must get through. You may have to strain it several times.

4. Into a large saucepan put the juice from the lemons, 900g of sugar and 1 litre of water. Heat gently to dissolve the sugar, but do not let the mixture boil. Add it to the strained ginger liquid *plus* another 2 litres of water.

Oct 5

5. The ginger beer is now ready for bottling. Pour it into clean bottles and seal them with *corks*. NEVER USE SCREW TOPS! Pressure can build up in-

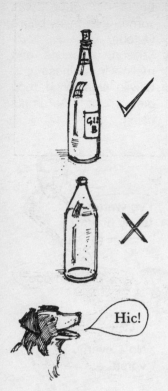

side the bottles, and a cork will pop out, but bottles with screw tops can explode. Not only is this dangerous, it will make you *very* unpopular!

6. Store the bottles somewhere dark and cool, like a garden shed, attic or cellar where nothing can get damaged by whizzing corks! Leave the ginger beer for *at least* 3 weeks before drinking.

7. When you want to make some more ginger beer, put just *half* of the solid yeasty material into a clean jar and start again adding the sugar and ginger every day for seven days.

Oct 6

A very famous poem about Autumn was written by John Keats, one of England's greatest poets. He died in 1821, when he was only twenty-six years old. Which of these is the first line of his poem?

a) I wander'd lonely as a cloud . . .
b) When the hounds of spring are on winter's traces . . .

Oct 7

c) Bright October was come, the misty-bright October . . .
d) Season of mists and mellow fruitfulness . . .
e) O wild West Wind, thou breath of Autumn's being . . .

Oct 8

I've written a funny poem.

An odd ode?

No – even verse!

Oct 9

Oct 10

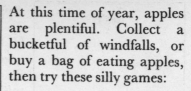

Oct 11

At this time of year, apples are plentiful. Collect a bucketful of windfalls, or buy a bag of eating apples, then try these silly games:

Apple Bobbing

Fill a large tub with water, nearly to the brim, and float apples in it. Competitors line up. On the word 'Go' they race to the tub and try to pick apples out with their teeth. They must keep their hands firmly clasped behind their backs. The first person to pick up an apple is the winner.

It's a very splashy game, so be careful where you play it! If you haven't got a tub, each player can have his or her own bucket and apple.

Swinging Apples

Make holes through the apples and thread each one on to a length of string. Tie the strings to a line (such as a washing line) at about head height. Players compete to see who can eat a complete apple first without using their hands.

Applesticks

Oct 12

Hide several apples in a big bowl of flour or sawdust. Players use just chopsticks to see how many apples they can lift out of the bowl. If you have no chopsticks, use the handles of wooden spoons. This is a very messy game!

Margaret Thatcher was born on October 13th. The surname Thatcher was probably given originally to people who thatched roofs. Many surnames are connected with occupations. Obvious ones are Baker and Butcher, but did you know that Fletcher means 'maker or seller of arrows', and Cooper means 'barrel-maker'?

Oct 13

Some surnames show where people lived. 'By' at the end of a name means 'place' or 'village' as in Appleby ('from the village of apples') or Danby ('from the place of the Danes'). Brook means 'dweller near a stream', and Moore means 'moorland dweller'.

MR. NIGHTINGALE

MR. SPRING

Mac, Mc and Ap, at the beginning of a name, mean 'son of'. Pritchard was once Ap Richard – 'son of Richard'. 'Son' at the end of a name means the same thing, as in Smithson, Jackson, Cookson, and so on.

Oct 14

People were sometimes named according to how they looked. The name Black might be given to someone with dark hair or skin. Nicknames were used, too. An active, nimble individual could be called Spring or Lively, while one with a sweet voice would be Nightingale.

Can you guess the meanings of these surnames?

BROWN, PROBERT, SADLER, RICHARDSON, CROSBY, SMITH, LONG, SHARP, MACARTHUR, MILLER

October 14th is the birthday of Cliff Richard, whose real name is Harry Webb. Perhaps his ancestors were weavers.

Mid-October each year sees the announcement of the *Nobel Prize* winners. The Nobel Prizes were created in 1901 by Alfred Nobel, a Swedish chemist.

Oct 15

One day, while lifting a bottle of highly-explosive nitro-glycerine from a box of fine powder, Nobel spilt some of it. It formed a paste with the powder. The mixture was still

explosive, but was much safer to handle in this form. Nobel had invented dynamite.

This invention made him a very rich man, and he used some of his fortune to set up awards for Physics, Chemistry, Physiology or Medicine, Literature and Peace. Later on, a prize for Economics was added.

Oct 16

Some people find it strange that the world's foremost prize for peace-making should be created by the man who invented dynamite, but Nobel set up the prizes to encourage work that would benefit mankind, to balance the harm that the invention of dynamite might cause.

Famous Nobel Prize winners include Martin Luther King and Mother Theresa of Calcutta (Peace), George Bernard Shaw and Sir Winston Churchill (Literature), and Sir Alexander Fleming (Medicine).

What prize do you get if you only have a knocker on your door?

The No-bell prize, of course!

Trafalgar Square in London, with its statue of Horatio, Lord Nelson on a tall column, commemorates the Battle of Trafalgar, which took place on October 21st, 1805, at Cape Trafalgar, on the southern coast of Spain. It was a great English naval victory, in which Admiral Nelson's fleet shattered the power of France and Spain and saved England from any chance of invasion.

During the battle, while on the deck of his flagship, *HMS Victory*, Nelson was hit by a musket shot from the French ship *Redoubtable* and died. His body was returned to England, pickled in a cask of brandy, and he was given a hero's burial in the crypt of St Paul's Cathedral.

It was at Trafalgar that Nelson signalled his famous message: 'England expects that every man will do his duty.' Already in conflict he had been blinded in his right eye and had lost his right arm. During the battle of

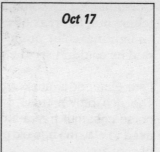

Oct 17

Oct 18

Copenhagen, his commanding officer sent him a signal telling him to break off action, but Nelson wanted to go on fighting, so he put his telescope to his blind eye and said he couldn't see the signal.

Late October is conker time. The rich brown fruits of the horse chestnut tree are often used to play the age-old game of conkers.

The best conkers are the hardest, and you can harden a conker by soaking it in vinegar for 24 hours, then baking it in a low oven for one hour. (Make the hole first, as it will be very difficult afterwards!)

Winning conkers are known as 'one-ers', 'two-ers' etc. according to how many victories they've won. The champion untreated conker of all time was a 'five thousand plus-er', which won the BBC Conker Conquest in 1954!

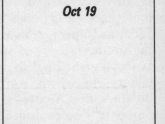

Oct 19

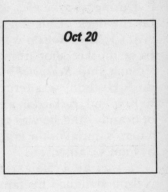

Oct 20

Oct 21

The 6 letters of the word CONKER can be re-arranged to form another 6-letter word. Do you know what it is?

If you were born between October 24th and November 22nd you are probably a forth-right type of person who strides boldly into the future. You may well be very amusing and entertaining. This is because you come under the star sign SCORPIO.

Famous Scorpio people include the actor Richard Burton, Robert Louis Stevenson and Ian Botham.

The Famous Five like the autumn, with its log fires and crumpets for tea. It's also a time for walking through woods and kicking up the leaves.

How many different types of tree can you find in this story? Underline them as you find them. (One's already done for you.) There are 12 altogether:

'IT'S TIME FOR A MEAL. I'M EVER SO HUNGRY,' DECLARED DICK. 'WE'VE GOT GIN-GER POP, LARDY CAKE

Oct 22

Oct 23

Oct 24

133

AND LASHINGS OF CHOCOLATE!'

'I THINK WE SHOULD WAIT TILL WE'VE STUDIED THE MAP. LET'S DO THAT FIRST,' ARGUED JULIAN, PACING AROUND THE CLEARING.

ANNE THOUGHT MAYBE HER ELDER BROTHER WAS RIGHT, BUT SHE DIDN'T WANT TO HAVE A ROW AND SPOIL EVERY-THING.

JUST THEN A PLANE FLEW OVER THE BAY. LOOKING UP, EACH OF THEM WAS SILENT FOR A MOMENT, THEN GEORGE SAID: 'I BET THEY'RE ON THEIR WAY TO THAT CAMP IN ECHO WOOD.'

Oct 25	*Oct 26*
Oct 27	*Oct 28*

Timmy, what is the outside of a tree called?

Bark!

There was a young person called Tonkers
Who went out to look for some conkers;
They fell on his head,
And though he's not dead,
I fear he's now totally bonkers.

Oct 29

Oct 30

October 31st is *Hallowe'en*, the time for ghosts and witches and dressing up in spooky masks.

Oct 31

The name 'Hallowe'en' comes from 'All Hallows' Even' – the eve of (or day before) All Saints' Day, which is celebrated on November 1st.

Some people (especially in the USA) make pumpkin lanterns and set them in their windows with candle lights inside, to scare away the demons.

If you can get hold of a pumpkin, cut a small circle out of the base and scrape out all the flesh and pips. Now use a sharp-pointed knife (*be careful!*) to cut triangles for the eyes and nose and to make a pointy-toothed mouth.

Place the pumpkin head carefully over a lighted candle that's been stuck to a saucer. (*Matches and knives can be dangerous*, so make sure you ask a grown-up for help or permission.)

Answers to October puzzles:
Page 125: d. Page 129: Having brown hair or skin; son of Robert; saddle maker; son of Richard; from the village with a cross (or crossroads); blacksmith; tall; clever or astute; son of Arthur; worker in a flour mill. Page 133: Reckon. Page 133: Lime, poplar, ash, maple, fir, may, elder, rowan, plane, bay, peach, pine.

NOVEMBER

Guy Fawkes, fizzing rockets, warm clothes, dark evenings and tea by the fire. What else does November mean to you? Time to be looking forward to Christmas – or perhaps it's your birthday month.

Nov 1

Lots of famous people were born in November, including Lester Piggott (5th), Olympic eventer Lucinda Green (7th), Prince Charles (14th), and Sir Winston Churchill (30th).

Nov 2

Try this **Famous Five November quiz:**

1. Anne is Uncle Quentin's N_ _ _ _.
2. Julian is O_ _ _ _ than Dick.
3. Anne, Dick and Julian like to V_ _ _ _ Kirrin Cottage.
4. In *Five on a Treasure Island*, Dick makes his E_ _ _ _ _ up a well shaft.
5. The Famous Five are good at solving them! M_ _ _ _ _ _ _ _.
6. The name of a hill where the Famous Five have an adventure. B_ _ _ _ _ _ _ _.

Nov 3

Nov 4

7. The first name of their creator.

E___.

8. Mr R_____ is the tutor in *Five Go Adventuring Again*.

Nov 5

Are you planning a firework party? What is your favourite kind of firework? Julian likes rockets, Dick likes Roman candles, Anne likes Catherine wheels and George likes bangers – and Timmy hates all of them! (Remember to keep animals indoors when there are fireworks around. *Never* play with fireworks. *Always* follow the Firework Code.)

Nov 6

As everyone knows, November 5th is *Guy Fawkes Night*. It's been celebrated for hundreds of years. Here's a very old rhyme about it:

Please to remember
The fifth of November
Gunpowder, treason and
plot.
We know no reason
Why gunpowder treason
Should ever be forgot.

Did you know that Guy Fawkes was not the leader of the Gunpowder Plot? He just happened to be the man on the spot when a search was made of the vaults under the House of Lords. The ringleader was Robert Catesby who, in 1605, planned to blow up the Houses of Parliament

Nov 7

and King James I. When Guy Fawkes was caught red-handed with the thirty-six barrels of gunpowder, he was tortured until he revealed the names of his fellow plotters. All were executed.

How many sticks are there in this bonfire?

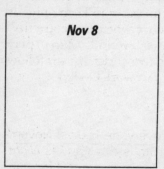

Nov 8

Here's a fireworks party recipe that is quite easy to make and really yummy to eat!

Aunt Fanny's Bonfire Crackles:

You will need:

25g icing sugar	25g cocoa
100g cornflakes	1 tablespoon golden syrup
25g margarine	12 paper cases

1. Set out the paper cases.
2. Sift the icing sugar and cocoa together into a basin.
3. Put the margarine and syrup in a saucepan over a low heat. Stir with a wooden spoon until melted.
4. Take the pan off the heat and add the sugar, cocoa and cornflakes to the melted mixture.
5. Place one heaped teaspoonful of the mixture in each paper case.
6. Leave to set for half an hour.

Did you know that by lighting just ten bonfires you could send a signal the length of Great Britain – from Land's End to John O'Groats? The Ancient Britons used these beacon fires to signal danger from an invasion.

Nov 9

November 11th is the *Feast of St Martin*. He was the Bishop of Tours, in France, and on November 11th in the year 380 AD, so legend says, he met a poor man who was very cold. He gave the man his own cloak, so God rewarded him by making the weather nice and warm until he could get him-

Nov 10

140

self a new one. The days around this date are often warm and sunny, and this is known as St Martin's Summer.

The second Sunday in November is *Remembrance Day*, when we remember those who lost their lives in the First and Second World Wars. Wreaths of poppies are laid at the Cenotaph in Whitehall, London, and at other war memorials. A two-minute silence at 11 a.m. marks the time of the signing of the peace treaty with Germany in 1918.

Nov 11

The poppies we wear are made by the Royal British Legion, and remind us of the battlefields of Flanders, in northern France, where much of the First World War fighting took place over fields where poppies grew abundantly.

Nov 12

The *London to Brighton Veteran Car Rally* takes place in November. A veteran car is one made before 1919, whereas a vintage car is one constructed between 1919 and 1930.

The rally starts at Hyde Park and finishes on the seafront at Brighton – a distance of approximately 50 miles.

Nov 13

Although a modern car could cover this distance in about an hour, the veteran cars take much longer.

Did you know that the first petrol-driven motor car was built by a German – Karl Benz – in 1885?

If you're interested in old cars it's worth going to see the

Nov 14

famous collection owned by Lord Montagu and kept at Beaulieu in Hampshire.

When cars from Britain are taken abroad they have an identification mark – 'GB'. If you saw these identification letters on the backs of cars, could you tell which countries they were from?
a) USA. b) ZA. c) BUR.
d) E. e) GBZ. f) NL. g) CH.
h) B. i) I. j) GR.

Nov 15

Nov 16

What kind of car does Timmy like best?

A Rover, of course!

No sun – no moon!
No morn – no noon
No dawn – no dusk – no
    proper time of day.

No warmth, no cheerfulness,
    no healthful ease,
No comfortable feel in any
    member –
No shade, no shine, no
    butterflies, no bees,
No fruits, no flowers, no leaves, no birds, –
    November!

Thomas Hood 1799–1815

NOVEMBER contains something Timmy likes, though. What is it? (It has four letters.)

How many other words can you find from the word NOVEMBER? There aren't very many:

....

....

....

....

....

....

....

....

Nov 17

Nov 18

Nov 19

Autumn Wild Life Quiz

1. Which black and white bird is supposed to be lucky if seen in pairs, but unlucky on its own?
2. One of these animals sometimes takes over part of a rabbit warren as his home. Is it a badger, a vole, a weasel, a squirrel or a fox?

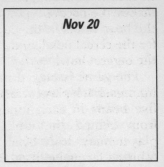

Nov 20

3. Red, fallow and Père David are all types of – what?
4. What do a toad, a dormouse and a hedgehog have in common?
5. The coat of a stoat goes white in winter. What is it called when white?
6. Is a water boatman a type of newt, a river rat, or a kind of insect?

Bean Tossing

This is a good game for a rainy day! You'll need some dried beans, some dishes, and a pencil and paper to keep score.

Nov 21

Place a cup inside a cereal bowl, then put them both inside a large bowl. Place this nest of dishes on a table, about one metre from the

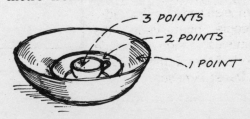

3 POINTS
2 POINTS
1 POINT

edge. The idea of the game is to throw the beans into the dishes. You score 3 points if the bean lands in the cup, 2 for the cereal bowl, and 1 for the biggest bowl.

The game is played in 10 innings. Each player can toss five beans in each innings, from behind the table. A player may lean over the table as far as he likes, but must not touch the table. Write down each score, and the winner is, of course, the person with the highest score.

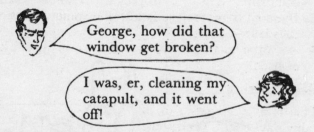

SAGITTARIANS (born between November 23rd and December 21st) are independent people, who hate to be tied to one place! If you can get them to sit still for long enough, however, you'll find them wise and kind-hearted.

People born under the Sagittarius sign include Woody Allen, Tommy Steele and Derek Jameson.

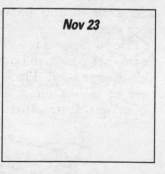

145

Nov 24

Nov 25

This is the time of year when Americans celebrate *Thanksgiving*. In 1621, the Pilgrim Fathers arrived in Massachusetts, on the East coast of the USA, having sailed from Plymouth, Devon, in the *Mayflower*. They founded a colony which they called Plimoth. Thanksgiving Day celebrates their first harvest.

The traditional meal eaten on the fourth Thursday in November in the USA is turkey with cranberry sauce, followed by pumpkin pie.

Nov 26

Julian invented this puzzle. Can you solve it?

What do these dates have in common – January 18th, February 26th, March 7th, April 15th, May 5th, June 22nd, July 3rd, August 2nd, September 1st, October 29th, November 26th and December 16th?

Nov 27

Why are greengrocers always popular?

Because they are never short of dates.

Nov 28

147

Nov 29

Is Timmy a Yuppie?

No, he's more of a yappie, really.

Nov 30

November 30th is the *Feast day of St Andrew*. The New Testament tells us that Andrew was a fisherman in partnership with his brother Simon Peter. Before following Jesus, he was a disciple of John the Baptist. He's the patron saint of Scotland.

Answers to November puzzles:
Page 137: **1.** *Niece.* **2.** *Older.* **3.** *Visit.* **4.** *Escape.* **5.** *Mysteries.* **6.** *Billycock.* **7.** *Enid.* **8.** *Roland. Page 139: Eleven sticks. Page 142: a) United States of America. b) South Africa. c) Burma. d) Spain. e) Gibraltar. f) The Netherlands. g) Switzerland. h) Belgium. i) Italy. j) Greece. Page 143: Bone. Also bee, beer, bore, born, ember, eon, eve, ever, even, me, mere, morn, more, no, nor, on, one, orb, ore, oven, rev, robe, roe, rone. (Can you think of any more?) Page 144:* 1. *Magpie.* 2. *Badger.* 3. *Deer.* 4. *They all hibernate in the winter.* 5. *Ermine.* 6. *A kind of insect. Page 147: If you write them like this: 18.1 (18th January), 26.2 (26th February), and so on, you'll find that in each case all the figures add up to ten. (1+8+1, 2+6+2 etc.)*

DECEMBER

The days are getting shorter, the weather's getting colder, and everyone begins to prepare for CHRISTMAS!

Did you know that many of our Christmas customs have pagan origins? Pagan sun-worshippers celebrated the winter solstice (the shortest day of the year – around December 21st/22nd), and the early Christians simply adapted the festival, rather than try to get rid of the ancient customs altogether.

In Northern Europe, as the days became longer again, they celebrated the return of the sun by burning yule logs.

Famous December birthdays include Frank Sinatra (12th), Kenny Everett (25th) and Tracey Ullman (30th).

The first Christmas cards were sent in Victorian times and were often very ornate. If you want to send a large number of cards this year, you could try this quick but effective design. All you need is thin card (or thick paper), a piece of Christmas wrapping paper, a packet of stick-on stars, scissors and glue.

1. Cut out and fold a piece of card or thick paper in half.
2. Fold the wrapping paper and cut out half a Christmas tree shape. Open it out.
3. Stick the tree to the front of the card.
4. Decorate the tree with stars.

If Christmas puddings are made at home, everyone in the household should take turns to stir the mixture with a wooden spoon. Tradition says that the pudding should be stirred in a clockwise direction, and a wish made at the same time. What is your Christmas wish?

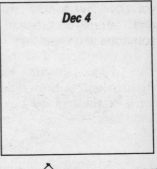

Dec 3

Dec 4

George, Julian, Dick and Anne like to make as many Christmas presents as they can. Home-made cakes and sweets make lovely gifts, and so do pictures – if you're good at drawing or painting – or decorated pencil pots. (Simply make a paper sleeve for an old jar and colour it or cover it with stick-on paper shapes!)

George is giving Aunt Fanny a huge lovespoon to hang in the kitchen at Kirrin Cottage. If you want to make a lovespoon for someone, buy an ordinary wooden spoon (any size you like) and carefully paint it with two coats of an oil-based paint. When the background coats are dry, paint on a design in one or more bright colours, perhaps incorporating the person's name or initial. Finally, add a coat of clear varnish.

Decorate your spoon by tying a ribbon around it, and you now have a really unusual and attractive present for someone you love.

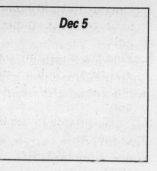

Dec 5

Dec 6

The Twelve Days of Christmas

You probably know this song, but here's a new way to sing it – with actions! See if you can get right the way through without falling over in a tangle.

Go right through the song from the first day to the twelfth, finishing up like this:

On the twelfth (*spread all ten fingers and touch ears with thumbs*) day of Christmas, my true love (*hands on heart*) sent to me

Twelve drummers drumming (*play imaginary drum*)

Eleven pipers piping (*play pipe*)

Ten lords a-leaping (*jump up and down*)

Nine ladies dancing (*twirl round quickly*)

Eight maids a-milking (*pretend to milk cow*)

Seven swans a-swimming (*make 'swan's neck' with one arm*)

Six geese a-laying (*'draw' egg shape with other arm*)

Five gold rings (*wiggle fingers of one hand*)

Four calling birds (*wave arms like wings*)

Three French hens (*'peck' with head*)

Two turtle doves (*make 'shadow picture' bird by crossing hands and thumbs and flapping closed fingers*)

And a partridge in a pear tree (*squat on one leg, as if roosting*).

Dec 7

(When you sing 'On the first', 'second', 'third', etc. 'day of Christmas', hold up the appropriate number of fingers. For 'eleventh', hold up ten fingers, touching one ear only.)

At the end of term, the Famous Five usually go back to Kirrin by train. This is a game they like to play on the way:

Dec 8

Wiggle-Wink

This is an 'action' version of the word game 'I Packed My Bag'.

The first person makes a particular movement (scratching his nose, for instance) and the next person must copy that action before adding one of his own. By the time you get to the fifth person, he might have to:

Scratch his nose
Pull his left ear
Wink his right eye
Wiggle his thumbs
Bite his lower lip

– the last being his own addition to the list. The others should watch very carefully, as any mistake in their copying of the actions (using wrong hand, winking wrong eye, etc.) means they are out of the game.

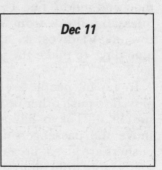

Wiggle-Wink-Whoosh:

This is the same as 'Wiggle-Wink', except that each player combines a noise with his action. Each noise should be as distinct as possible from the others (e.g. squeaks, growls, creaks, laughs, various animal noises).

Dec 12

Dec 13

Dec 14

Did you know . . .

The longest railway journey you can make without changing trains is six thousand miles? The Trans-Siberian railway, from Moscow to Vladivostok, takes nine days to make the journey.

In Japan, people are employed to push other people on to trains! The Shinjuku station in Tokyo has about eighty train-pushers to shove the passengers in. In the winter-time, extra pushers are hired, because people wear thicker clothes, so it's more difficult to cram them in!

Dec 15

Can you unscramble these strange phrases to find the names of some Christmas carols?

LENT IN SIGHT
AY, AN EARWIG MAN
WHERE GET SINK

Dec 16	Dec 17

The Famous Five are making paper chains. Two of them are holding the ends of the same chain. Which two?

In *Five Go Adventuring Again*, Julian, Dick, George and Anne decorate the Christmas tree.

Christmas trees were not introduced to Britain until the 1840s, when Prince Albert, the husband of Queen Victoria, made them popular. However, the bringing of evergreen branches into your house to ward off evil in the

Dec 18

coming year had been a custom in Europe for many centuries.

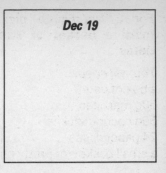

Dec 19

Every year the people of Norway send us a large Christmas tree, which is set up in Trafalgar Square. It's a present to the people of Great Britain, to thank them for their support of Norway during the Second World War.

Plant your own Christmas tree in a bucket of wet earth, or support it in a special stand that keeps its base under water. Remember to top up the water every day, and you should find your tree keeps its needles right up to Twelfth Night.

When decorating your tree, hang the lights on first. The Famous Five always get an adult to check the lights and make sure they're safe and working properly.

Dec 20

If you want to make your own baubles, it's not too difficult. You'll need ping-pong balls, a needle and thread, glue and coloured glitter powder.

1. Carefully make a small needle hole in a ping-pong ball.

2. Dip the end of a length of thread into the glue and push it through the hole. Leave it until the glue is dry.

3. Now paint the ball with glue and shake glitter powder over it. For a really professional effect, you could first decorate the ball with enamel paints, then add the glue and glitter wherever you want it.

For a last-minute present, make a **basket of stuffed dates**:

You will need:
a box of dates
50g marzipan
50g coconut flakes
24 paper cases
a small basket (or pretty box)

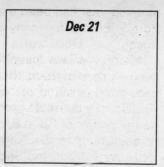

1. Split each date and take out the stone.
2. Press a piece of marzipan into each date.
3. Tip the coconut into a bag and drop the dates in one by one, shaking the bag to ensure each date is covered in coconut.
4. Place each date in a paper case and arrange them in the basket.

If you were born under CAPRICORN (December 22nd to January 20th) you are a bit of a worrier. You should try to look more on the bright side!

Famous Capricornians include David Bowie, Ludwig van Beethoven and Muhammed Ali.

Does Santa Claus leave his sleigh on the ground or on the roof!

Woof!

Dec 24

Dec 25

It's here at last! Happy Christmas!

December 26th – *Boxing Day* – gets its name from the old tradition of hanging up boxes in churches for offerings to be dropped in for the poor and needy. These boxes were opened and distributed on the day after Christmas.

Pantomime Quiz

In which pantomimes would you find:

1. A character called Dandini?
2. A cow sold for a bag of beans? Jack & Beanstalk
3. A widow who runs a Chinese laundry?
4. A cat whose master becomes a Lord Mayor?
5. A cat who kills a giant?

Dec 26

6. Robin Hood and two lost children?
7. A spinning wheel?
8. A talking mirror?
9. A very large white bird?
10. A hungry wolf?

Dec 27

If you have any Christmas pudding left over, put some out for the birds – they'll love it. (Don't do this with pudding that's been too well soaked in brandy, though, or your garden will be full of hiccuping robins!)

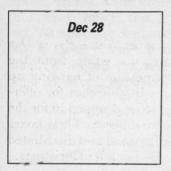

Dec 28

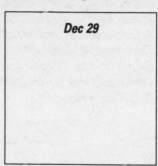

Dec 29

December 30th was the birthday of the great Walt Disney, whose animated films continue to delight audiences all over the world. His most famous cartoon character, Mickey Mouse, was 'born' in 1928.

December 31st is New Year's Eve. If you're having a party, you might like to make some **Famous Five Fizz**:

This makes a big jugful. Take one can of fizzy orange, one can cola, one can lemonade, half a bottle apple juice, mix all together in a jug and cool in the fridge!
    Happy New Year!

Dec 30	Dec 31

Answers to December puzzles:

Page 154: 'Silent Night', 'Away in a Manger', 'We Three Kings'. Page 155: Anne and Timmy. Page 158: 1. Cinderella. 2. Jack and the Beanstalk. 3. Aladdin (Widow Twankey). 4. Dick Whittington. 5. Puss in Boots. 6. The Babes in the Wood. 7. The Sleeping Beauty. 8. Snow White and the Seven Dwarfs. 9. Mother Goose. 10. Little Red Riding Hood.